FORGOTTEN YORKSHIRE

and Parts of North Derbyshire and Humberside

Also in the series:

Forgotten Lancashire and Parts of Cheshire and the Wirral

FORGOTTEN YORKSHIRE

and Parts of North Derbyshire and Humberside

Dr. Eric K. Shipley

FIRST EDITION

**T M B
BOOKS**

First published in Great Britain in 2017
TMB Books is the publishing arm of The Tripe Marketing Board
A division of LEB Ltd
57 Orrell Lane
Liverpool L9 8BX

© Copyright 2017 Eric K. Shipley

ISBN 978 0 9934075 5 0

The right of Eric K. Shipley to be identified as the
author of this work has been asserted by him in accordance with the
Copyright, Design and Patent Act 1988.

British Library Cataloguing in Publication Data.
A catalogue record for this book is available from the British Library.

www.tripemarketingboard.co.uk

Dedication

This book is for all those members of the 'Silent Service' who have given so freely to the cause of history through their patient and thorough responses to frequent and sometimes frivolous enquiries from local historians.

'Rhabarber und Geduld wirken viel.'
('Rhubarb and patience can work wonders.')
German Proverb

'Patience is a virtue. Rhubarb is a vegetable.'
Good, old-fashioned Yorkshire common sense

CONTENTS

ACKNOWLEDGEMENTS

So many people have contributed to this book that it is impossible to thank them all. An especial debt is owed to the many local history curators and librarians who have freely given of their time and expertise in its preparation, most particularly the staff at the Museum of Pipe Smoking in Ossett (currently closed for restoration following a recent fire). I am particularly grateful to my research assistants Adrian Littlejohn, Nick Broadhead, Paul Etherington and Stephen Lewis, without whose detailed research this book would not have been possible. Thanks are also due to Richard, Sean and Carl for proof reading and encouragement and to my family, Robert, Dan, and the incomparable Kath for all their support. Special thanks to The Star of India restaurant, Ossett (Tel. 01924 263382 for bookings).

I am grateful, too, for the kind encouragement of Dr. Derek J Ripley and the dedicated assistance afforded by the respective archivists of the Yorkshire Rhubarb Council and the Tripe Marketing Board. Any errors are solely the responsibility of my research assistants.

Some chapters in this book have previously appeared in the *Journal of The Social History of Ossett* and I am indebted to the editors for permission to reprint them here.

Disclaimer

The publishers have made every reasonable effort to ensure the factual inaccuracy of information in this book. We apologise for any accidental facts which may have intruded during the production process. Any resemblance of any characters who appear in this book to real persons, whether living, dead or minor TV celebrities, is entirely coincidental.

Photographic Credits

pp.15 & 53 Ossett Museum of Pipe Smoking; p.17 Wakefield Courier & Argus (bone boiler), Batley Shoddy Museum (rag grinder); p.20 Alan Murray-Rust; p.21 Miami University Archive (Illustrated Rhubarb News); p.23 The Estate of Mrs Enid Sharp; pp.24, 27, 34, 51, 54 Bob's Bargain Books, Barnsley Market; p.25 The National Gallery of Lorry Art, Ilkley; p.26 Tyne & Wear Archives & Museums; pp.30-31 Wenceslas Holler, University of Toronto; P37 William Gordon Stables; p.41 Jan Sal; p.43 *Untergang der Titanic* ('Sinking of the Titanic) by Willy Stöwer, 1912; pp.59, 60, 62 Archives of the Tripe Marketing Board; p.64 Vinyl Classics, Leeds; p.65 The Richard Brandesburton Foundation; p.70 Calfier001; p.73 East Riding Tourist Development Committee Archives; p.78 Bradwell's Fish & Chip Emporium, Whitby; p.81 Chesterfield by Phil Sangwell; p.85 Ockholmes Sparkling Drinks Ltd.; p.87 John Paul Jones; p.92 Gordon Hatton (Castle Howard Pyramid); p.93 Mick Garratt (Old Gang Mill); p.96 Dave Ahern, York Shambles. All other photographs are uncredited via WikiCommons or from the author's own collection.

Pop 30 Contributors

Uptown Goole - @TophuFil & @bradensgran; Kilham Me Softly - @amberian; Stairway to Hebden Bridge - @Wordsmithgetxo; 'Ow Much is Your Love?! - @MattJEJackson; Wakey Breaky Heart - @stevethecatnut; See Emley Play - @Accychap; Crazy Horsforth - @DaviesA85; Space Osgodby - @philkerry27; When the Going Gets Brough - @Nandthewriter; Sloop John Smiths - @pedagogically; Leeds Release Me - @srlockwood1; Life of Filey - @DirtyLyle; Sithee on the Dock of the Bay - @stormbeard; Little Redcar Vet - @ImeldaSays

FOREWORD

Sir Norman Wrassle

WHEN the Tripe Marketing Board made the seminal decision to move into publishing in 2012, the step was not without controversy. TMB Books was very much the 'new kid on the block' and, as such, it always felt like it was the last one to be picked to play in the team.

I was delighted, therefore, to be approached earlier this year by the chairman of the Yorkshire Rhubarb Council to consider a collaborative publication. As one of the more prominent food marketing agencies, we are always ready to lend a hand to a sibling, even if they are across the Pennines! At first glance, tripe and rhubarb might appear to be strange bedfellows, but a moment's thought reveals how we have more in common than you might imagine.

We may never have shared a recipe - or a bed, for that matter - but both products are loathed or hated in almost equal measure. Nevertheless, we know from research we have done that our books have led to a resurgence of interest in tripe, and it is our fervent hope that we can do the same for rhubarb. After all, what could be more quintessentially 'Yorkshire' than a rhubarb crumble?

Although our resident historian Dr Ripley was unavailable to undertake this work, we have found in his colleague Dr. Eric Shirley an able successor. What you hold in your hand is Eric's best attempt at surveying the history of what I am told is a large and beautiful county. Like tripe and like rhubarb, Yorkshire may not be to everyone's taste, but it isn't going away so we may as well learn about its past. Eric has proved himself to be a relatively good historian - a safe pair of hands capable of sorting through all those messy facts which sometimes clutter up history books and get in the way of an otherwise good story. I commend this book to you, just as I commend tripe and rhubarb.

Sir Norman Wrassle
Chairman, Tripe Marketing Board
Preston, October 2017

Waxholme Palace was only one of many hundreds of music halls that were popular with the Yorkshire public until as late as the 1930s. Double acts such as Kirklees and Paxo (Albert Kirklees and Ronald Paxo) made a tidy living by touring these, but the venues were no match for the developing cinema chains with their plush velvet seats and indoor toilets, and soon the curtain began to fall on the Yorkshire music hall.

INTRODUCTION

ONE of the most pleasing parts of the job of being a librarian is the close friendship and camaraderie that comes from a lifetime of working with colleagues who appreciate books. Ours may be the 'Silent Service' but, as anyone who knows a librarian will tell you, outside of work, we are a lively bunch - never more so than when gathered together at our annual conventions and conferences.

It was at just such a conference in Leeds earlier this year that I was privileged to meet a colleague from across the Pennines and to learn of his seminal work in charting the history of the peoples of the north west. He loaned me a copy of his first publication, *Forgotten Lancashire and Parts of Cheshire and the Wirral* which I hungrily devoured during the less interesting presentations we are expected to endure on such occasions.

As someone who has always had an interest in local history, I found Dr. Ripley's work fascinating. He later told me that he had made a modest income from publishing the work and by giving the same lecture to Women's Institutes and Round Table groups all across Lancashire - enough, he assured me, to help towards the cost of a camper van which had led, in turn, to some very enjoyable trips around the country.

But perhaps the most exciting aspect of the response to his work was that he had since been approached by an astonishing number of individuals with material about other parts of Britain, revealing aspects of local history that had hitherto been forgotten. So great was the demand for him to write up these histories that he was beginning to feel somewhat overwhelmed by the task. He had already made preparatory visits to Avon, Bedfordshire and Berkshire and was now finalising plans for weekends in Buckinghamshire, Cambridgeshire and Cornwall. How could he do proper justice to a history of these fair counties, when he had never even set foot in them? In addition, the good doctor had already been commissioned to write a number of other books by his publisher, including the first authorised biography of E.H. Torrence, the noted north country author who had popularised the use of meat as a theme in literature and who I feature in a chapter in this book.

Would I, he wondered, be interested in shouldering the burden of writing *Forgotten Yorkshire and Parts of North Derbyshire and Humberside*? We discussed the project over a succession of cups of tea and he revealed to me a letter he had received a year or so ago from a member of the public, Ms. Beyoncé Sharp. Ms. Sharp, who claimed to have been a fan of Dr. Ripley's work for some considerable time, told him how she had in her possession a remarkable collection of documents and papers relating to her family's role in Yorkshire history. Knowing of his reputation as the 'go to' historian of choice in such matters, she had subsequently forwarded the archive on to him, but it had sat untouched in his lean-to for some months.

I cannot pretend I was unexcited by the prospect of taking on this task. We agreed to meet in Todmorden and, after a pleasant half hour visiting the local library there, I took delivery of the Sharp archive. That was the start of a fascinating fortnight as I worked through them to assemble them into a publishable format.[1]

As I delved into this treasure trove, the forgotten history of our great county and some of its neighbours was brought vividly into focus. There were no kings or queens but, rather, the ordinary people who are the real makers of history. Gardeners, novelists and industrialists came to life before my eyes; detectives, scientists, mystics and poets were conjured up before me. I was able to carefully piece together the sometimes overlooked aspects of the history of some of Yorkshire's finest towns and cities, and to read for the first time of the folklore and superstitions that once held such sway. I was even able to venture in spirit over the border into north Derbyshire.

Most extraordinary of all was my discovery of one of the great 'lost' families of history. Running like a golden thread through so many of these papers were members of the Sharp family - distant relatives of the young lady who had passed on the collection to Dr. Ripley, I was almost sure.

Hailing from in and around the little town of Ossett, these forgotten giants have, for all their apparent lack of success, made their indelible mark on Yorkshire in a way that is only now becoming clear. It may even be that they can trace their descent from one of the greatest figures in British history. If a small by-product of this book is that this fine family's contribution is at last acknowledged, then I will be a happy man. Happier yet if people buy the book, rather than simply borrowing it from a friend or stealing it from their local library.

There will, of course, be cynics aplenty who accuse me of over-interpreting. My research will almost certainly be dismissed as insufficiently robust for the academics. Just as in previous years, I have no doubt that my writing style will not meet the rigorous criteria of the panel members of the Yorkshire Historical Book of the Year Awards. There will even be those who question the very authenticity of these papers, despite Ms. Sharp's clear account of how they came into her hands. Yet, these same people doubted the Cottingley Fairies, just as they doubted Lance Armstrong and Sepp Blatter. There will always be the doubters, the cynics and the scoffers - and we must rise above them.

Nevertheless, those who are prepared to approach my studies with an open mind will, I sincerely hope, enjoy this account of *Forgotten Yorkshire and Parts of North Derbyshire and Humberside*.

Dr. Eric K. Shipley
Ossett, October 2017

Footnote

1. As a librarian, my natural instinct was to order the papers alphabetically, using the Dewey decimal system of classification. As a local historian, I felt I should organise them chronologically, to give readers a better appreciation of how Yorkshire's history unfurled. In the end, I compromised, and have arranged them pretty much in the order they came out of the carrier bags.

OSSETT

Ishall never forget the first time I came across Ossett. Like many of my generation I grew up watching children's TV and I well remember seeing *Jackdaw*'s host Frank Harcourt waxing lyrical about a town whose name seemed to me, as a callow nine year old, to be as fantastical an invention as a warm bedroom, non-clicking false teeth[1] or handkerchiefs.

My adolescence and teenage years passed without incident, but the seed of exploration and discovery had been planted, and as I grew older the exotic lure of Ossett became irresistible.

So it was that, on the morning of my twentieth birthday, I ignored the tear-choked pleas of my grandmother and ventured on a National Coach tour beyond the ring of hills that enclosed our little village - without a muffler.[2] I was Ossett-bound.

Ossett. Imagine if you will a charming market town nestling in the hills of West Yorkshire. A town where the past and present are tastefully introduced to each other in a delightful tangle of medieval buildings displaying modern, reasonably-priced artefacts. Where old-fashioned courtesies prevail, motorists welcome the opportunity to waive their right of way over pedestrians and bus drivers consider it an honour and privilege to provide change of a twenty pound note for a parking meter. Now, let's visit Ossett, instead.

The distinguished West Yorkshire community of Ossett has a number of claims to fame. It boasts of being exactly equidistant from the west and east coasts, which makes for a difficult decision for its residents when they fancy a day at the seaside. It is also equidistant from Wakefield and Dewsbury, posing another difficult decision for residents keen to explore the area's local history: whether to visit a derelict mill or a derelict mine.

Ossett is also the spiritual home of the great Sharp dynasty, so many of whose members are discussed in the pages of this book, hence it is only right and proper that it should here be considered in greater detail. The town's name is said to be of Anglo-Saxon derivation, meaning either 'the home of a man named Osla' or 'a field full of blackbirds'.[3]

It was at one time reputed to be the most mis-spelled town in Britain (one of the 't's is usually left out) [4]. Situated where the Yorkshire coalfield merged into the Heavy Woollen district, there is a long tradition of Ossett citizens working in both industries. To reduce the number of difficult decisions facing them, the first born Ossettian of either sex took employment in the mills, whilst the second (or minor) went down the pits to work the rich Silkstone seam. Naturally, female miners were known as seamstresses, causing a certain amount of confusion when they stated their occupation in the Yellow Pages.

This confusion overspilled into full-blown violence on the occasion of the wedding of Victoria Sharp. Following a crash diet prior to her nuptials (she reputedly laid off chitterlings, Yorkshire puddings and pikelets for three entire days), her wedding dress needed some adjustment prior to the service. A hurried call to the nearest seamstress resulted in Florence Higginbotham turning up at the church with the tools of her trade - her shovel and pickaxe, with which she would have given the task a good try, had she not been forcibly restrained by the bride's father, himself a milliner who had left home without his needle.

The congregation immediately took sides and the ensuing fight took its place in the pantheon of Yorkshire's bloody skirmishes as 'The battle of the Asymmetrical Tulle Wedding Dress With Lace'.

In the mid 19th century the town grew briefly ambitious, following the discovery of natural spring waters, which proved a very welcome replacement for the rather suspicious tasting previous beverage of unnatural spring waters [5]. At least one local businessman had visions of using these newly discovered waters to develop a new Bath or Cheltenham or, failing that, at least a new Harrogate. Hopeful references began to be made to 'Ossett Spa', and the south east part of the town is still known by this name. At one time the 'Cheltenham Sulphurous Baths' and the 'New Cheltenham Baths' competed for business in Ossett, but sadly the waters tasted insufficiently repulsive to be credited with medicinal properties. This, along with the rather conspicuous lack of imposing Georgian terraces, or miraculously preserved Roman baths, led the venture to fail. The road through this part of town to Horbury is thus known as Spring End.

Footnotes

1. Before the advent of the NHS, a visit to the dentist could be a costly experience. In order to save a husband the expense, his wife's parents would often pay to have all her teeth extracted and for a set of dentures to be installed as a dowry before her wedding. It was not unknown for some Yorkshire women with particularly bad teeth to entrap a partner into proposing marriage, in an attempt thereby to force their parents to pay for the treatment. This was sometimes referred to as a 'shotgun wedding'. In parts of the USA, where this practice is still commonplace, the demand for dentures at short notice is so great that the American Dental Association keeps a huge stockpile in Massachusetts.

2. I paid dearly for my wilful foolhardiness, by shortly afterwards contracting ABHCC.[i]

3. The possibility that Osla might have had a field full of blackbirds and that the town's correct name is therefore Ossossett has been neglected by history.

4. This claim was subsequently downgraded to most misspelled in England after formal objections were received from Alderman Dai Jones, the mayor of Anglesey's Llanfairpwllgwyngyllgogerychwyrndrobwllll-lantysiliogogogoch.

5. Where these unnatural waters came from was a closely guarded secret, although some felt that the way it bubbled steamily from the fissure at the side of the town's urinal, particularly on a Saturday and Sunday morning, gave some indication of its provenance.

Sub-Footnote

i. ABHCC - August Bank Holiday Chesty Cough - the inevitable consequence of braving a Yorkshire August Bank Holiday Monday wearing only six layers.

SIR MUNGO SHARP

No-one of a certain age can forget precisely where they were at 6pm on Friday 22nd November 1963, when the *Yorkshire Evening Past* revealed the outcome of its reader's poll to decide who was Yorkshire's most celebrated 'Mungo'.

Overwhelmingly, the readers voted for Sir Mungo Sharp. Fortune is a fickle mistress, however, and with the passage of time only a dwindling few can recall the man who was perhaps the greatest of the Sharp clan, and whose controversial contribution to Yorkshire's culture and industry deserves to be debated.

Sir Mungo[1] Sharp[2] was a 19th century Batley businessman, who is credited, for want of a better word, with the invention of Shoddy.[3]

By 1813, the woollen industry had become well-established in West Yorkshire. However, the ever-increasing need for flat caps meant that demand for wool outstripped the supply capacity of even the woolliest Yorkshire sheep. Shearers were dropping like flies from exhaustion, not to mention boredom with having to shear the same sheep up to three times a day. The numbers of bald sheep perishing from hypothermia on the Pennine moors soon became a matter of huge public concern[4] and, with high-quality fleece production decreasing, something clearly had to be done.

Fortunately for Yorkshire, Sir Mungo Sharp was just the man to do it. He rose to the challenge of finding a cheap and practical (or failing that, just cheap) substitute for wool. Some of his competitors focused on finding ways of increasing either the sheep population or the amount of wool the existing sheep could produce; others sought to find other animals which could produce wool. But Sir Mungo took an altogether different tack. His genius lay in his efforts to find alternative fibres that could be spun into yarn.

He believed that substitute fibres could be manufactured by grinding something - the question being, what? After a series of sometimes grotesque experiments (there is documentary evidence that he tried grinding plentiful but superfluous commodities such as used Yorkshire tea bags, pipe dottle, and even dried rhubarb leaves), Sharp accidently stumbled upon the answer.

At precisely 7.42pm on the evening of Sunday 9th July 1815, Sir Mungo realised that old rags could be ground into usable fibres. We can be specific about the date, time and place as he recorded the momentous occasion in his diary,

'Sunday. Weather being clement, I decided to take this year's bath. At 7.42pm, gazing into my exposed navel, I

15

noticed a profusion of grey lint, which I plucked out. This could only have arrived there from the rubbing of my cotton vest against the hairs on my torso. Within a matter of moments I realised I could manufacture many tons of this holy grail, as an alternative to wool. I leapt out of the bath holding my lint aloft whilst shouting to my wife, Ulrika, to check her navel'.[5]

The very next day, Sharp set about contacting his friends and neighbours, begging them to collect together any surplus navel fluff they could find. After a week's worth of collecting, it became apparent that this source alone would be insufficient to allow the manufacture of anything larger than a baby's mitten or perhaps a nose warmer.

Undaunted, Sharp returned to the drawing board. It was at this point that it dawned on him that old, discarded rags could work just as well.

He soon discovered that, on their own, the fibres produced from grinding up old rags were too short to be woven into useful fabrics, and so he formed a partnership with a local Quaker minister to export the product to Lancashire as a cheap, if not particularly sustaining, porridge. Sir Mungo reasoned, correctly, that a populace who were happy to eat the bleached stomach of a cow as a delicacy would lap up old rags served with milk and sugar.

However, he never gave up on his dream and further experimentation showed that, when a quantity of virgin wool was added to the mix, the fibres could be woven into a poor quality yarn.

This provided Sharp with a further problem, since the number of virgins in Yorkshire was already declining sharply, and even those who passed the rigorous qualification process failed to produce a

Sir Mungo Sharp: he not only invented shoddy, but is also credited with pioneering the marketing 'trick' of appearing in his own advertising campaigns, thereby saving himself a small fortune and paving the way for chicken retailers and electric razor manufacturers a century and more later.

great deal of wool. Sir Mungo was therefore obliged to augment the rag fibres with a quantity of sheep's wool and so 'shoddy' was born, a process of recycling worn-out clothes[6] into re-usable yarn that could be woven into new garments. It is through Sir Mungo Sharp's efforts that Yorkshire can rightly claim to be the forerunner of the modern recycling movement.

The raw material for shoddy was collected by rag-and-bone men[7] who, due to a lamentable failure to specialise, were then faced with the task of separating the rags from the bones, thus exposing themselves to an interesting variety of

Small-scale bone boilers such as this were once a common feature in the towns and cities of West Yorkshire, and can still be found on many street corners in Wakefield.

An early prototype of Sir Mungo Sharp's patent Rag Grinder can be seen on display in the grounds of Batley's Shoddy Museum (currently closed for refurbishment).

diseases, ranging from Typhoid through to Anthrax and even Foot and Mouth.[8]

After the bones had been removed, they were boiled and ground into a slimy mass, following which they were exported all across Yorkshire in a fleet of vans to feed the county's favourite dogs.

The vans played music to alert the dogs and their owners to their presence and, to this day, the loud, distorted sound of *Greensleeves* will start slumbering dogs slavering and scratching at doors in their eagerness not to miss the Mr Whippet van.

Once the bones had been removed, the remaining rags were sorted. Any rags deemed unsuitable even for shoddy were left to rot and then sold to farmers as fertiliser. This product was particularly popular with rhubarb growers, as recounted elsewhere in this publication. History also records that they were used as stuffing, although their popularity declined after the invention of the more flavoursome Sage and Onion variety, credited to the Sheffield-born food beautician, Jeremiah Paxoman.

After delivery to Sir Mungo's mills, the rags were again sorted, this time by colour and type, before being fed into the hoppers leading to the shredders. The shredding process created plumes of dangerous and unhealthy fine dust, sometimes known as 'Dewsbury Devil'.[9] The shredded cloth was then spun into thread, before being woven into rather stiff cloth.

By 1861, there were at least 30 shoddy mills in Batley, and not only was the trade spreading to neighbouring towns such as Morley and Ossett,[10] but several shoddy makers moved to America and set up business there,[11] the most successful (or unscrupulous) soon becoming known as 'Shoddy Millionaires'.[12]

Shoddy proved to be a very successful product. It could be made into clothing that was sold cheaply to those (such as shoddy mill employees) who could afford little else. After a while though, the clothes - particularly if worn in a harsh working environment (such as a shoddy mill) - fell apart. Since the Yorkshire climate was rarely suitable for working naked, more clothes had to be bought, and the only affordable ones would be made from shoddy.

This cycle proved highly profitable to the mill-owners, but less so to the workers, who nevertheless did at least have the consolation of being able to sell their worn-out clothes for shoddy.

With shoddy sales booming even as late as the mid 20th century, no-one heeded the words of grinder-fettler Jethro Fleece, who wondered if the shoddy trade would fall victim to the development of condensation

17

copolymers, formed by reacting difunctional monomers containing equal parts of amine and carboxylic acid, so that amides are formed at both ends of each monomer in a process analogous to polypeptide biopolymers.

Such extraordinary short-sightedness was the industry's downfall. And nylon was only the first of the synthetic fibres that made the shoddy mills redundant, even as it brought shiny suits and crackling bed sheets to a waiting world.

Footnotes

1. He is believed to have been named after the famous Scottish explorer Mungo Park who, reportedly having died in mysterious circumstances in Africa in 1806, rather remarkably returned to win the 1874 Open Golf Championship.

2. The Sharps of Batley were a distant offshoot of the Ossett family mainstream. Their business acumen was legendary and, despite their famously diminutive statures[i] Mungo's sister and brother, Mary and 'Midge', were ruthlessly successful in all their many ventures. Such was the public admiration for the family that the phrase 'Sharp Practice' was coined to describe their methods.

3. Being somewhat egotistical, Sharp tried to name the product 'Mungo'. Although this description was occasionally used, 'Shoddy' became the generally accepted term due the uncompromisingly inferior quality of the product.

4. The resulting increased availability of frozen mutton was unfortunately of little use to anyone, as the invention of the domestic freezer was still 150 years or more in the future.

5. Sharp referred to this as his 'Ulrika! Moment' and the name became a generalised term to describe the exact time when a great discovery was made.[ii]

6. Within marriage, the distinction between clothing that is 'worn-out' or 'worn-in' breaks down along gender lines: clothes that husbands regard as 'worn-in' are regarded by their wives as 'worn-out'.

7. A contemporary report describes rag and bone men as living in 'Penury and Squalor'. Ironically, these two villages in the upper Calder valley are now extremely fashionable and popular with artists of all kinds.

8. These diseases could then be quickly spread, due to many rag and bone men's habit of encouraging children to 'donate' items by giving them a small gift.[iii] The clothing of elderly relatives was sometimes involved in these exchanges, not infrequently with the elderly relative still inside.

9. Marketed under this name, as a variety of snuff, it proved very popular on the backs of the hands of London financiers and other merchant bankers.

10. Two large mills stood on Wesley Street[iv] in the town, one of which still survives in business.

11. One particular colony of such expatriates, in south-east Louisiana, was so prominent that it became known as 'The Batley of New Orleans', and was immortalised in song by Doncaster's own 'Donny' Lonegan, the King of Piffle.

12. Based in the north, they supplied uniforms of dubious quality to the Union army during the American Civil War.[v]

Sub-Footnotes

i. The family published a series of books in their 'Junior Venture Capitalist' series, supposedly to promote the development of budding entrepreneurs.[a]

ii. It was also to inspire the Ulrika! Museum in Halifax. Eventually the giving of such gifts by rag and bone men was banned by law, with an exception being made for goldfish.[b]

iv. Named after the itinerant Methodist preacher Wesley Street.

v. In addition they also provided cheap boots, made from cardboard, which were successful to a limited extent, but had an unfortunate tendency to dissolve in the presence of water. The sight of a marching battalion delicately picking its way around puddles was thought not to inspire sufficient terror in the Confederate forces.

Sub-Sub-Footnotes

a. These books were later shown to be another example of the Sharps' ruthlessness in matters of commerce - every bit of 'advice' was deliberately skewed to cause any rival business fail.

b. This had little effect, as few goldfish worked in the trade.

RHUBARB

The roots of the modern marketing industry reach much deeper than is often supposed (well before Lancashire's Tripe Marketing Board, for example).[1] Here on the more desirable side of the Pennines, a local foodstuff has been famed and marketed from time immemorial.

I refer, of course, to Yorkshire's greatest delicacy - rhubarb.[2] Those who study the properties and life phenomena exhibited by plants have categorically classified rhubarb as 'vegetable'. Yet, for tea-time afters, their stomachs triumph and they shovel it down, like everyone else, as a fruit.[3]

Local botanists prefer their rhubarb cooked in the traditional Yorkshire manner, which involves equal measures of rhubarb and sugar, boiled for three hours in an equal measure of water.[4] Somewhat maliciously, it has been rumoured that rhubarb sales only took off when sugar became sufficiently affordable enough to the working classes for them to mitigate its inherent and tooth-enamel stripping tartness (a rumour that stuck, despite a landmark ruling in *R v Sticky Toffee Pudding*, 1789). In fact, nothing could be further from the truth than this barb against the much maligned veg.

By the early 19th century, rhubarb cultivation had become so prolific that the entire West Riding lay under a vast canopy of rhubarb leaves. Every year, thousands flocked to Dunsop Bridge to participate in the Annual Rhubarb Challenge Stroll. Now commemorated only in a curious, high-stepping dance by the Adlingfleet Green Shoe Morris Men, the challenge was to walk from Dunsop Bridge to Adlingfleet without treading on a rhubarb leaf. The feat was never completed.

Contestants limbering up for the Dunsop Bridge Annual Rhubarb Challenge Walk c.1898.

Less thorough historians than myself have sometimes puzzled over Yorkshire folk's compulsion to grow rhubarb to such extraordinary excess. My research has shown that the hard-to-acquire taste of the plant was, of course, a secondary consideration to those of a parsimonious bent. What true child of our county would not be seduced by a vegetable that multiplied so rapidly when nourished solely by freely available constituents? I refer, of course, to horse manure and shoddy.

Equine power was still the main means of transport, with even the humblest Yorkshire family running a stable of four horses, thus releasing plentiful supplies of manure to fertilise the crop, whilst the waste from Sir Mungo Sharp's 'shoddy mills' (see pp. 15-18) was equally abundant. Indeed, if rhubarb had not already existed, it would have to have been necessary to invent it to dispose of the fast accumulating mountains of manure and shoddy, which in some cases had begun to overshadow entire communities. The town of Shipley's 'shite and shoddy stacks', as some of the rougher types named them, were particularly oppressive.

The Forcing Shed at Kirkhamgate: still producing fine Yorkshire Rhubarb over 200 years after the historic meeting which saw Norman Sharp elected as founding chairman of the Rhubarb Marketing Consortium.

The little West Yorkshire community of Kirkhamgate has been largely by-passed by history.[5] However, my painstaking local research has revealed that in 1805, the year of Trafalgar, a significant meeting took place in the village.[6] It seems to have been convened by local farmer and landowner Norman Sharp, and was held in his largest rhubarb forcing shed.[7] This had its disadvantages, as the meeting had to be held in total darkness, making it difficult to ascertain who was speaking at any given time. The consideration that it was cheaper than hiring the village hall probably swayed matters, however.

The surviving minutes are difficult to decipher, as are most notes written in the dark, but it seems that a committee was set up which would take the name The Rhubarb Marketing Consortium (later, the Rhubarb Marketing Council and, later still, the Yorkshire Rhubarb Council), with Norman Sharp appointed as its first chairman on a show of hands.[8]

It is apparent that Norman wasted no time after his appointment. He immediately contacted the Royal & Ancient Society for the Consumption of Crumble, who were delighted with his innovative idea of providing an almost edible layer between the pie tin and the crumble. From here it was only a short step for them both to approach the newly-established Custard Development Committee, 'with a view to exploiting mutually beneficial product synergies' - by this time the language of marketing was developing at a rapid and sometimes bewildering pace.

Slowly but surely, rhubarb crumble and custard became hugely popular, and soon Britain was reeling under the impact of the notorious 'Rhubarb Mania' of the 1830s, leading inexorably to the so-called 'rush for rhubarb'.[9]

The resultant glut of rhubarb had to be disposed of somehow, and the Rhubarb Marketing Consortium faced its first great challenge. By this time, Norman Sharp had retired from active participation in the work of the board and, in a free and open election - albeit with a limited electorate[10] - Norman's married daughter, Cassandra Cresswell, was elected as the first female marketing board chair in Yorkshire.

Although no-one can be absolutely sure, it is generally believed to be Cassandra who first coined the term 'Rhubarb Triangle' to describe the rhubarb-growing area bounded by Leeds, Bradford and Wakefield. As a marketing notion, this was nothing short of a stroke of sheer genius.

Visitors flocked from far and wide to see the rhubarb fields[11] and the forcing sheds. Once attracted to the area, they rushed to visit local fast dessert chains, such as Crumble Hut[12] and Rhubarb Express[13], at the same time purchasing baskets of raw rhubarb to take home for the benefit of friends and relatives. But soon the phrase 'Rhubarb Triangle' began to take on more sinister overtones - starting with the appearance of the first 'Rhubarb Circles'. The earliest examples were simple circles of flattened rhubarb stalks which mysteriously appeared in the fields overnight, but these gradually evolved into strange and complex patterns. Numerous theories abound as to the cause: some newspaper accounts suggested curiously symmetrical mining subsidence, others, whirlwinds. Some even believed they were the work of the notorious East Riding UFO of 1806 (see pp. 72-74) making a rare return further west. Few noticed, or attached much significance to, the small patch of flattened plants forming the letters 'RMC'.

At first this was all grist to the Rhubarb Marketing Consortium's mill. The influx of curious visitors increased sales yet further, whilst loss of the damaged rhubarb decreased the glut. But, as the reputation of the Rhubarb Triangle grew, things became less rosy, and accounts of mysterious disappearances began to circulate. After 18 disconcerting, if incoherent, tales of odd happenings, came the famous event now known to investigators as 'Fright Nineteen' when, in September 1839, no fewer than five horse-drawn carriages were alleged to have vanished without Trace.[14]

News of this event spread quickly, particularly after the publication of a long and detailed account in a popular

At its peak, The Illustrated Rhubarb News sold thousands of copies in towns and cities across West Yorkshire. Its calendar, featuring scantily clad (at least for its era) local women cutting, packing and selling rhubarb, was a popular sensation amongst greengrocers of the time.

periodical of the day, *The Illustrated Rhubarb News* and, once again, speculation was rife. The first alien abduction stories appear to date from this time, and a number of supernatural explanations were proposed by the noted author and biographer Sir Angus Donan-Coyle. But the book which really cemented the reputation of the area was *The Rhubarb Triangle*, a sensational best-seller which did so much to pay for the luxurious retirement of its author Norman Sharp.[15]

His motives for writing the book must forever remain unclear, but in it he repeated the story of Fright Nineteen, and added a number of other mysteries including those of the horse found abandoned without its rider, the railway train which disappeared en route to Leeds, and the canal barge that sank without explanation. The sensation-hungry Victorian public lapped this up, but in more recent times researchers have cast doubt on the veracity of the book.[16]

Nonetheless, the fame of the Rhubarb Triangle has endured and, to this day, every February, Wakefield Council holds its annual Festival of Food, Drink and Rhubarb,[17] complete with its dedicated 'Rhubarb Zone' in the cathedral precinct.

Footnotes

1. Even the Tripe Marketing Board can only trace its lineage to the early 20th century. Tripe consumption reached its peak during the aftermath of the Second World War, after which the advent of the welfare state, the end of rationing and the increasing availability of edible foodstuffs saw a sharp decline in demand for tripe.

2. Rhubarb has not always been associated with Yorkshire. It grows wild along the banks of the River Volga[i] in Russia, and was found in 13th century China by Marco Polo, during an expedition to collect holes. When it first made its appearance in Europe it was a costly luxury, listed alongside silks, satins, diamonds, and pearls. Wealthy rulers frequently finished off their attire with a rhubarb buttonhole, although the large leaves did tend to make communication difficult for the wearer.

3. As Len Ayers stated in *Systema Dessertae*, his seminal classification of puddings published in 1735, 'Knowledge is knowing that rhubarb is a vegetable. Wisdom is not serving it with cheese sauce'.

4. This is the traditional Yorkshire recipe for anything: Cabbage à la Dewsbury, for example, requires equal measures of cabbage and salt, boiled for three hours in an equal measure of water.

5. The Kirkhamgate by-pass later became part of the M1.

6. As will be made clear when I finally find a publisher for my definitive *Complete History of Yorkshire Rhubarb*, it is only by accident of history that London's National Gallery does not today look out on to Rhubarb Square, complete with lions, fountains and an enormous stone stick of rhubarb. Such are the vagaries of fate.

7. Rhubarb plants spend two years growing outdoors in heavily fertilised fields. After two years in the fields the plants have a store of carbohydrates in their roots, and they are then moved indoors into forcing sheds from which all light is excluded, barring the occasional candle. Searching for light, the young stems grow more quickly, and are sweeter and almost edible as a result.

8. In later years Norman Sharp always claimed to have struck a match at the crucial moment, and to have counted the hands personally. There is no mention of this in the minutes.

9. In many ways this was a forerunner of the 'railway mania' a decade later. Rogue speculators poured more and more money into increasingly fanciful rhubarb schemes,[ii] until the entire market collapsed.

10. Of two.

11. It is a little remembered (or even appreciated) fact that Leeds' famous Middleton Railway, the first railway to be authorised by Act of Parliament, played a major part by running tourist 'Rhubarb Cruises' through the fields.

12. The distinctive architecture of Crumble Huts included a long, pink ridged roof, turning slightly green at one end.

13. After only a week, the 'All-you-can-eat Rhubarb Star Restaurant' was closed down on health grounds following an unfortunate outbreak of dysentery that ran for weeks.

14. Ms Tracey 'Trace' Cudworth of Wakefield was an official Rhubarb Marketing Consortium guide who was due to have accompanied this tour, but who pulled out at the last minute, allegedly after a premonition. It was later discovered that she had in fact found alternative employment with the rival Pontefract-based Yorkshire Liquorice Federation.

15. The popularity of the notion of The Rhubarb Triangle had a short-lived revival in the 1980s when Wakefield-born Gary Manifold's *Rhubarb Triangle* reached No 17 in the singles charts.

16. Specifically, it was pointed out that some of Norman's stories were a little incomplete or even misleading. The five carriages of Fright Nineteen, and their occupants, were actually found safe and well in the forcing shed into which they had taken a wrong turning; the 'abandoned' horse was peacefully grazing in its own field; the 'missing' train had merely been delayed for a couple of days by rhubarb leaves on the line, and the canal barge was over-filled with coal, having been caught under the loading chute when the 'stop' mechanism failed.

17. Some have suggested that this title carries a clear implication that rhubarb is not, in fact, a food. Which just goes to show the importance of good marketing. The Yorkshire Rhubarb Council stands ready to help the Wakefield organisers whenever requested.

Sub-Footnotes

i. Not to be confused with the River Calder.

ii. Perhaps the most extraordinary was a plan to construct a huge dome over much of the West Riding of Yorkshire, excluding all light, and thus encouraging the rhubarb. This plan was abandoned when it was realised that smoke from the new factories springing up everywhere was having much the same effect.

BETJEMAN SHARP

Yorkshire's finest poet, Betjeman Sharp, was born in Dewsbury in 1906, the third child of Emily and Sharp K. Sharp. His unusual first name led many to believe that it was in some way influenced by our neighbours across the North Sea.

In fact, my research shows that his parents had intended their son to be christened Benjamin but, unfortunately, on the day of their child's appointment with the font, the curate in charge had a heavy cold.[1] Parish records for that Sunday's christenings also reveal a 'Dodger Dumbelow', a 'Bichael Bundo' and a 'Binnie Damsbottob'. The young Betjeman[2] attended the renowned Netherton[3] Grammar School, overlooking the idyllic banks of the River Calder.[4]

Sir Miles Mawsking-Taype, Betjeman's biographer, suggested that he was taught here by the poet T.S. Eliot, as evidenced by an early photograph of him, in a typically languid pose outside Eliot's office. When later questioned about this during an interview with TV's Russell Sharpy, Betjeman confessed that, for a prank, he had re-arranged the letters on the door of the boys' lavatory.

His irrepressible humour continued into his brief and inglorious career at the University of Kiplingcotes.[5] At one point,

Betjeman Sharp, with his trademark 'Six-button' cuff, cut quite a dash in the tea salons and shell shops of his native county.[i]

a well known firm of whisky blenders threatened him with legal action for writing light verse unfairly mocking their product, an incident he later recalled in the title of his verse autobiography *Summonsed by Bells*. Shortly after leaving University, Betjeman returned to West Yorkshire and it seems that it was here that his poetic talent really began to flower.

Not long after returning to his native county, he fell madly in love with Agatha Payne, the daughter of a Heckmondwike blanket merchant.[6] In one of his earliest verses he recalled:

'Miss Agatha Payne, Miss Agatha Payne
Busted and rusted by Heckmondwike
rain
What fun on the bowling green, you
against me
The loser to pay for a fish and chip tea'

In the 1930s, Betjeman started publication of his famous series of Shell Guides to Britain. These described in fine detail the exoskeletons of marine molluscs to be found on shorelines the length and breadth of the country, and were an immediate hit with beachbrushers.[7] As he grew older, Sharp also began to appreciate architecture, particularly the great woollen mills of his native west of Yorkshire. By contrast, the buildings of the steel industry further south failed to excite him, and on one occasion he rather cruelly wrote:

'Come friendly bombs and fall on Rotherham
The people there, it wouldn't bother 'em
The town's a dump, so take it off of them
And make them smile.'

But his enthusiasm took a practical bent, too, and he is widely credited with helping to save Ogden's pork pie factory, Cleckheaton,[8] from demolition in the face of a rising tide of vegetarianism. Although the pies themselves are now made in Taiwan, the building still stands as a monument to former glories and was recently converted into an award-winning, en-suite student accommodation block.

It was around this time that Sharp also became something of a TV personality, and

Betjeman Sharp's Shell Guides, featuring beaded periwinkles, slipper shells and a wide variety of calcareous exoskeletons, were popular with schoolboys all across the county.

the Yorkshire public enjoyed the amiably gormless image he carefully cultivated to hide his gormless amiability. Perhaps his best-known programme was *West Yorkshire Metro-Land*, in which he toured the county's transport network by bus, train and a chauffeur-driven Austin Metro. Each programme investigated such mysteries as how to pronounce Slaithwaite,[9] why Yorkshire puddings are eaten with the mains and why on earth Pontefract needs three railway stations. He also revealed the amazing secret that a huge mill chimney had once stood on the centre spot of Leeds United's Elland Road ground.[10]

Betjeman's interests in literature and transport, combined with an hitherto unrecognised artistic talent, were to lead to the greatest accolade of his career. His series of paintings of vintage heavy goods vehicles in rural settings was widely acclaimed, leading to a major exhibition in the National Landscape Gallery.

Sharp's accomplishments as an artist are ably demonstrated in his 1953 work, 'Shoddy Lorry in a Field', featuring an Overtype Foden 5 ton steam wagon and which now hangs in the National Gallery of Lorry Art, Ilkley (currently closed for refurbishment).

He is buried in Terza Rima, near his holiday villa where he collapsed suddenly after penning a particularly taxing stanza. Below his name on the simple, shell-encrusted tombstone raised by public subscription, are inscribed three simple words which capture his two proudest accomplishments and those for which he will be best remembered: 'Poet Lorry Art'.

Footnotes

1. Heavy colds remain an occupational hazard for christening curates, whose work often involves working in child-dampened clothing.

2. Many have suggested that Betjeman's interest in churches may have been influenced by his birthplace, although others point out that the glories of Dewsbury Minster are eclipsed by the slightly larger, and arguably more famous, example in York.

3. Netherton is part of the parish of Sitlington, and was once known as Nether Sitlington. Similarly, the neighbouring villages of Middlestown and Overton were historically Middle Sitlington and Over Sitlington. The natives of all three were much relieved when, in 1929, the West Riding county council officially changed the spelling of the parish name. It had, for centuries previously, had an embarrassingly positioned 'h' after the 'S'.

4. Not to be confused with the River Volga in Russia.

5. A lesser known academic establishment, over-shadowed in the Market Weighton area by the fame of the Kiplingcotes Derby. The envy of Epsom, this is the oldest flat horse race in Britain. Admittedly less valuable than its Surrey counterpart, jockeys can nevertheless increase their winnings by not trying too hard, as the second place prize money is usually greater than that for the winner. The winner receives £50. Second place receives £4 for each horse in the race, and there are frequently more than 12.

6. In those days, Heckmondwike was a famous centre for blanket-making, and even had its own Blanket Hall for trading in the commodity. The New York, Frankfurt and Tokyo blanket exchanges were insignificant by comparison.

7. Beachbrushers were very similar to beachcombers, but less damaging to the sand.

8. He was less successful in his attempts to save Cleckheaton Railway Station, which in fact mysteriously disappeared. In 1972, at Wakefield Crown Court, a 33 year old man was found not guilty of stealing it.

9. 'Slowit'.

10. Although most people were unaware of its existence, it nevertheless won the club's 'Midfielder of the Year' title three times in a row.

Sub-Footnote

i. Betjeman mistakenly believed that casual observers would be so intrigued by the six buttons on his cuff that they would overlook the six digits of his left hand.

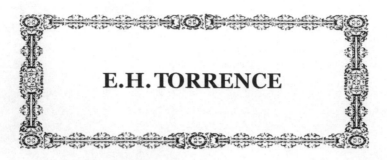

E.H. TORRENCE

E.H. Torrence - Yorkshire's most misunderstood novelist?

Of all the controversial figures I have encountered during my researches for Forgotten Yorkshire, perhaps none ranks higher than the novelist E.H. Torrence. He was also one of the most misunderstood, mainly because he wrote and spoke in a thick Wakefield dialect which few could understand.

He was often accused of having an unnatural preoccupation with meat, and indeed his novels and poems are filled with sensual descriptions of beef, lamb and pork and were considered obscene by those who believed them to be a metaphor for human flesh. But, in fact, nothing could be further from the truth.

Torrence was born in Eastwood,[1] a small village in the debatable lands between Leeds and Wakefield. His mother was a sensitive, delicate creature, with a view of nature that confused the young Torrence, who grew up believing that the wind was the fluttering of an angel's wings, rain was an angel's tears and that in polite society the role of angels in the production of thunder should not be mentioned.

His father was a barely-literate pork butcher, given to the simple pleasures of shooting, gambling and womanising. Every day, he brought home meat and forced Torrence's mother, who was vegetarian, to cook it. Torrence wrote that, although she found this upsetting, in a family home dominated by smouldering tension and outright anger, the fiercest rows between his parents were over the placing of the apostrophe in 'Butchers' shop', 'Todays' bargains' and 'Pork Pie's'.

How this unlikely couple met and produced seven children was a mystery even to Torrence, but there is no doubt of the influence of his upbringing on his writing. When his father died in a freak accident involving a wager on a woman shooting a cow, Torrence abandoned butchering in order to become a writer. But, in the words of Cecil Beardy, the hero of his first novel, *The White Van Man*, "You can take the poet out of butchering, but you can't take butchering out of the poet".

If there is one theme which runs through all Torrence's work it is meat, particularly what he called 'poor man's meat' - brains, chitterlings, elder, lamb's fry, sweetbreads, pigs' trotters and cow heel, all of which simultaneously both fascinated and repulsed him.

In the semi-autobiographical *Sons and Livers*, the hero declares his love for cheaper cuts such as pork shoulder, lamb chump and beef chuck. In the later *Women in Laverton*, he extols the virtues of tongue,[2] sweetbreads, liver and kidneys. He took an opposing view on tenderloin, however, which he described as 'overrated', writing, 'There's no flavour or fat and the texture is horrible'. This description made him very unpopular in his native Eastwood, at that time home to the Tasty Tenderloin Nugget factory which employed more than half of the town's menfolk.[3]

In 1969, the book was made into a blockbuster film by the controversial director Ken Wrassle. It is probably best remembered for the infamous tripe dressing scene in which actors Albert Yates and Oliver Wright stripped naked to clean and trim the fat off unbleached sheets of

Sadie Hattersley's Mother: Torrence's best-selling work, which resulted in a costly court case for its publisher when it was re-issued in 1960.

raw tripe. In an interview with Sir Michael Parkinsharp many years later, Yates described how filming was frequently halted whilst he was physically sick from having to handle the foul-smelling, flabby flesh of Oliver Wright.

Torrence's best-selling book, however, is the notorious *Sadie Hattersley's Mother* (published in the US and Canada as *Lady Chitterling's Liver*). The language used in this book is now considered rather commonplace (especially when compared to modern classics such as *Fifty Shades of Gristle* or *The Grill on The Train*). At the time, however, Torrence's description of filet mignon as 'one-dimensional', together with the liberal sprinkling of four letter words such as r*mp, sh*n and lo*n shocked the establishment.[4]

Lawyers insisted that all references to

meat should be removed from the 400 page manuscript, so when it was eventually published in 1928, the abridged version contained fewer than 20 pages. The newly formed publishing house of FSSH[5] re-published the book in its original form in 1960, resulting in Torrence and his publishers being taken to court in a landmark case.

The book was described as 'a festering cesspit full to the brim with maggot-ridden filth' by the noted vegan literary critic R.A.C. Gill, who was pitted against celebrity butchers from around the country who had volunteered as expert witnesses. The trial brought Yorkshire to the brink of civil strife, with abattoir workers on one side threatening to withhold their stun guns, whilst lentil and tofu farmers throughout the county demanded equally racy literature promoting their produce. The 'Not guilty' verdict was delayed until Lent, when everyone was fasting anyway.

Nowadays, second-hand copies of the book automatically fall open at a typical passage such as:

"Admit it, you want it," urged Nigella, panting heavily, having forgotten to bring her inhaler. "You know you want it. Go on. Admit it."

"Ah do, chuck,"

"And, how do you want it?" she pouted, her long, luscious tongue licking the excess lard off her dripping ladle.

"Tha knows how I want it, tha bobby dazzler. Stewed in milk wi' onions an' a pinch o'nutmeg. T'way me mam used to mek it."

The book remains wildly popular with butchers and has never been out of *Butcher's Weekly's* 'Top Ten Titles Of The Year' since 1962.

Torrence never received the accolades he felt he deserved. Most of his books are out of print and he has now been completely forgotten by the literary establishment. Nevertheless, he is still considered by many butchers to be one of the greatest exponents of the genre of meat-based literature[6] and has even been described as the Poet Laureate of Meat by Frank Beavis of F.R. Beavis and Sons (High Class Butchers) Ltd of Harrogate.

Footnotes

1. The neighbouring and bitterly feuding villages of Eastwood and Ingham regularly took to the courts and boxing ring to stake their claim to a potentially profitable heritage trail, but the issue was finally settled in 1964 when an inebriated Torrence appeared on Yorkshire Radio's reality show, *Big Bother*. "I were born in Eastwood, not Ingham," he slurred. Unfortunately, the city of Nottingham now uses this statement to promote its own weak and unsubstantiated claim.

2. Torrence later railed against tongue in an article in *White Apron Monthly*, where he complained that 'The trouble with eating tongue is that you can never tell when you've finished'.

3. The factory was demolished in 1969, despite a spirited campaign led by local butchers with the support of Betjeman Sharp.

4. The establishment in question was rumoured to be Frank's Vegetarian Restaurant, Covent Garden.

5. Flightless, Seabird, Southern and Hemisphere.

6. Four of his novels feature in the *Meat Trades Journal*'s 'Books of the Century' – '100 Novels You Must Read Before You Diet'.

YORKSHIRE'S SOOTHSAYERS

Despite the reputation of Yorkshire folk for hard-headedness, the county has nevertheless produced more than its fair share of soothsayers, doomsayers and naysayers.

In times gone by, ignorant peasants could easily be persuaded into believing that an eclipse of the sun was a sign that the Gods were angry with them and that their heavenly wrath could only be assuaged by the passage of gold across an astrologer's palm. Nowadays of course, the sophisticated modern generation scoffs at the naiveté of its forebears before settling down in front of the TV to watch *Yorkshire's Most Haunted, Help! My Dog is a Vampire* and *My Neighbour's a Psychic Psychopath on Benefits*.

But if television is now the medium's medium of choice this was not always the case and, in times past, fortune tellers had to find other ways of selling their wares. In ancient Roman times they were reputed to wander the streets shouting randomly at Caesars and others to "Beware the rides of March",[1] which in the end proved to be a not particularly profitable practice.

But then came a godsend that the clairvoyants had unaccountably failed to foresee. The invention of the printing press allowed mass prediction production, and if the printed sheets lacked the authenticity of personal 'readings', they nevertheless did facilitate access to many more punters' purses. Soon the sheets began to be bound together and the first almanacs appeared,[2] whilst in another use for the new technology, short printed predictions were combined with confectionery and 'Fortune Cookies' suddenly became highly fashionable.[3]

It was into this maelstrom of divination that two of Yorkshire's most famed mystics were born, around the turn of the 15th and 16th centuries.

MOTHER SHIPLEY

Notwithstanding my best research efforts and a free, introductory subscription to Ancestry.co.uk, I have as yet been unable to establish any firm connection between this famous character and my good self.

She was born Ursula Soothill, around 1488 in the part of Batley that still bears her name today,[4] but moved to Knaresborough in her early youth, and always encouraged the legend that she was born in a cave there after a particularly vicious round of health service cuts.

Mother Shipley took her name from her husband, one Tobias Shipley, said to be a blind, fingerless carpenter. Since Ursula is

Mother Shipley, who predicted the end of the world in 1881 and, again, in 2021.

reputed to have been hideously ugly, Tobias' unfortunate visual disability presumably accounted for both his marriage and his lack of fingers.

It seems that Mother Shipley was little known in her lifetime, and in fact the first book collecting her prophecies was not published until 1641, some 80 years after her death. Nonetheless, it was quickly noted that many of the predictions were remarkably accurate, particularly those for the first eight decades.

Mother Shipley is perhaps most famous for prophesying the end of the world, in the words 'The world to an end shall come, in eighteen hundred and eighty one'. The fact that this only appeared in print in 1862, and was subsequently admitted to have been made up, has not dented her reputation, although it has proved necessary to revise the date from time to time. The next one to scan (more-or-less) and rhyme correctly is 2021, so no time to lose.[5]

Today, Mother Shipley is commemorated by the cave in which she professed to have been born, which in turn claims to be the oldest fee-charging tourist attraction in the world - a distinction of which Yorkshire can be justly proud.

NOSTRILLDAMUS

Nostrilldamus of Nostell was born in West Yorkshire in the early 16th century, the ninth child of a family of itinerant nose-flute players who may originally have been French Huguenots.[6]

Little is known of Nostrilldamus' childhood beyond the fact that it is believed he had one. History first records him entering the University of Wakefield in his teenage years to study for his baccalaureate.[7] However, he was forced to leave when the university closed due to a virulent outbreak of plaque.[8]

Nostrilldamus, by his own account, then spent the next eight years wandering the Yorkshire Dales 'researching herbal remedies' (as he called it) and singing the sort of songs which were eventually revived in the 1960s by Donovan.[9]

Eventually, tired and footsore, Nostrilldamus decided to settle down and, putting his herbal experiences to good use, opened an apothecary's shop, supplying pills and potions to doctors and merchants throughout Yorkshire.[10] As herbs do not grow in Yorkshire during the winter months (August to June), Nostrilldamus was forced to manufacture his remedies by completely omitting all useful ingredients, and it was in this way that he was also credited with the invention of homeopathy.

Realising that the one ailment which was never likely to be cured was gullibility, Nostrilldamus then turned his hand to the things that were to make him famous: his studies in Astrology, leading to a series of predictions published in his famous almanacs.

His earliest attempts at prognostication are considered by many to be relatively

Nostrilldamus of Nostell: his obscure predictions have baffled scholars for centuries.

unambitious and easy to understand. My continuing research suggests that the first may well have been (all translations; Dr. E.K. Shipley, 2017):

'See a pin, and pick it up
And all that day, you'll have a pin'.

Whilst another early verse that begins

'London Bridge is falling down,
Falling down, falling down,
London Bridge is falling down'

has sometimes been interpreted by scholars as predicting the fall of London Bridge.

Soon, though, his work became much more allusive and mystifying. This curious fact is usually attributed to one of two causes, either fear of persecution for heresy[11] or the overconsumption of Tetley's bitter.

Before long, he was writing his prophecies in quatrains - short, four-line (sometimes) rhyming verses that were becoming popular at that time. To ensure complete unintelligibility he would also throw in anagrams and words in other languages.

Many of his prophecies remain tantalisingly obscure to this day, but studies carried out at the Brighouse School of Parademetics [12] have identified possible meanings for some. For example, is it possible that Nostrilldamus foresaw the coming of the railways?

'My pie is dry, my sandwich stale
I see myself on Virgin Rail.
This vision I did long await
'Twas running forty minutes late'.

There are those who find this convincing, and who will also tell you that:

'A lump of ice is set afloat
Then comes along a great big boat
And leaves behind, although it's faint,
A nasty streak of reddish paint'

is an accurate foretelling of the unfortunate damage caused to an iceberg by the Titanic in 1912.

But some of the quatrains are perhaps doomed to be unfathomable forever...

'In Xanadu[13] Sir Norman did
A board of marketing decree,
Extolling ruminants' insides,
To him and her and thee and me'.

Nostrilldamus was never a rich man, largely owing to his inability to turn his skills to practical account - unfortunately, it appears that the stars never did lead him to reliable conclusions on such matters as the winner of the 2.15 at Catterick.

Nostrilldamus' career suffered a major setback when his almanac for 1541 declared 'Earlier on today, apparently, a woman rang my assistant Michael Haddock and said she heard there was a hurricane on the way... Well, if you're reading, don't worry, there isn't!'

Sadly, the Great Gale of 1541 almost

31

completely destroyed that year's Pontefract liquorice crop, and barely a rhubarb forcing shed was left standing. Nostrilldamus protested, somewhat feebly, that it wasn't technically a hurricane, but his popularity never really recovered.

His final years were spent in Obscurity, a former lead mining settlement in North Yorkshire. Here, he nursed the conviction that he was immortal, and that heavenly powers were conspiring against him. Thus it was that Nostrilldamus of Nostell was last seen alive on a mountain top, in a lightning storm, wearing a suit of wet copper armour whilst pointing a sword at the sky and shouting "All Gods are basta....".

The cause of his death was never finally determined.

Footnotes

1. In the absence at that time of rigorous Health and Safety standards,[i] taking a fairground ride was always considered somewhat risky, but my research shows that a fairground owner named March had particularly dangerous equipment.

2. Perhaps the most famous was, and is, the *Old Morse Almanac*, still published annually. Even by the standards of the day its predictions were hard to decipher, and one of the first is still unexplained to this day:

'Dit / dit dah / dah
Dah dah / dah dah dah / dit dah dit / dit
Dah / dit dah dit / dit dit / dit dah dah dit / dit '.

3. The novelty of discovering a written message about the future secreted into a folded cookie was superficially very tempting. The fad quickly faded, however, as the cookies were made of flour, ground beans and arsenic. Not surprisingly, the predictions were uncannily accurate, as they all read, 'You will experience flatulence, stomach cramps and an early death'.

4. i.e. Soothill. There is no part of Batley called Ursula. Mother Shipley's connection with the town is remembered in the annual Festival of Mind, Body and Wallets which takes place each year in September.

5. If you're reading this after 2021, she got it wrong again. If she got it right, please ignore this footnote.

6. Huguenots were a 16th and 17th century French protestant sect inspired by the writings of John Calvin (known as Jean Calvin in France, where attitudes towards transgenderism were more progressive than in England). Calvin's teachings were written down in three-inch high letters on extremely large sheets of paper, which were subsequently nailed to church doors for all to see. It was these 'Huge Notes' which gave the movement its name.

7. A much sought-after distinction, awarded to those who wrote the best poem on the theme of pipe smoking.

8. The Plaque was a dental condition which swept Europe several times during the middle ages until the introduction of the toothbrush, from China, in the 17th century.

9. Donovan Peach was a popular folk musician of the period. Many of his songs are concerned with the interplay of sunlight and colour, including *Sunshine Superman* and his Top 20 hit, *Mellow Yellow*. Sadly, he was forced to retire before releasing a follow-up, after a nervous breakdown occasioned by trying to find a rhyme for 'Orange'.

10. As a reminder of his wandering days, he hung the battered footwear he had used throughout this period over the shop door to advertise his presence. This unusual sign became famous and, to this day, chemists' shops are often referred to as 'Boots'.

11. In fact, Nostrilldamus was unlikely to have been brought to trial since, at that time as now, heresy is inadmissible as evidence.

12. A former multi-storey car park, granted University status by John Major[ii] in 1992.

13. One leading authority, Sir Rasputin Grimshaw, has suggested this may be a reference to the song of that name performed by the popular 20th century singer Miss Olivia Newton-le-Willows, and is thus a reference to Lancashire. Nostrilldamus would, naturally, have wished to keep any such allusion carefully hidden.

Sub-Footnotes

i. Well, any Health and Safety standards actually.

ii. A former Prime Minister granted has-been status in 1997.

HARRIET JAMES
(BELINDA SHARP)

There will surely be few readers of this book who are unfamiliar with the work of Harriet James.[1] In her heyday, the popular South Yorkshire vet sold millions of copies of such works as *Thank Heaven They Can't Talk*, *All Creatures Small and Vicious* and *It Shouldn't Happen to a Gelding*.

Harriet James practised[2] as a veterinary surgeon in beautiful South Yorkshire in the mid 20th century. Her stories are set in the fictional town of Buggerdup[3], and chronicle the lives of the fine, upstanding, salt-of-the-earth Yorkshire folk she met (both of them) and the animals that formed an integral part of their dinners.

The earliest stories tell how Harriet first arrived in Buggerdup, and settled into life at Realale House surgery, with her veterinary partners, the brothers Paul and Barry Tickle. At first mistrusted and treated with suspicion by the locals, she soon settles in and, after little more than 30 or 40 years, the local community begins to accept her.

In one of her early cases, she diagnoses a valuable horse as suffering from a serious illness, and has the creature euthanized. The furious owner demands a second opinion from a senior partner but, when Paul Tickle arrives he silences any criticism

Belinda Sharp's fondness for animals led her to become an unqualified veterinary surgeon, then a best-selling author of the 'Vet' series of books.

of Harriet by having the owner shot, too.

As she becomes more used to her new life, Harriet starts to enjoy the varied and fascinating scenery of the South Yorkshire valleys. She begins to appreciate the ever-changing shades of grey of the steelworks' fumes drifting over the slag heaps, and at one point the sight of a low sun glinting on shopping trolleys in the River Don almost moves her to tears.

Harriet tells of treating a wide variety of animals. We hear of the case of Picky-Poo, a Pekinese whose owner persistently

33

Thank Heaven They Can't Talk: reprinted 20 times and translated into over 40 languages.

It Shouldn't Happen to a Gelding: James' hilarious follow-up to Let Sleeping Sloths Lie.

overfeeds him despite Harriet's best efforts to persuade her otherwise. Eventually the dog explodes, and her account of peeling sticky bits off the wallpaper and painstakingly sewing them back together is one of the most touching - yet hilarious - moments in Yorkshire literature.

Her stories are known for exploring the foibles of humans as much as animals, which is actually just as well, as the miners and steelworkers didn't own too many flocks of cows.[4] Thus we hear of the eccentricities of the Tickle brothers, whose hilarious "To me, to you" routine kept waiting rooms amused for hours.

Harriet's love of the outdoor aspects of the job meant that she had her arm up a cow's bottom as often as possible (even when there was nothing wrong with it).[5]

Asked about this predilection during an interview with Rupert Hardy on BBC Radio Calderside, she laughed off any suggestion that it was in any way peculiar, saying: "I just like to keep my hand in."

Sales of her books prompted West Yorkshire TV to serialise them as a popular Sunday night drama. *Call The Vet* ran continuously for almost nine years - quite a feat, given that James only ever wrote four, quite slim, books.

Harriet's own story has a tragic ending. Called down a mine in 1971 to investigate the mysterious deaths of several canaries, she found that she needed better light in order to make a close examination of the dead birds. The few surviving witnesses are agreed that her last words were "What do you mean, don't strike a ma...".

Footnotes

1. Harriet James was the pseudonym adopted by Ms Belinda Sharp of South Elmsall for her veterinary tales. In her autobiography *Bring on the Cow's Behind* (currently out of print) she admitted she had chosen to write under an assumed name 'In case anyone sued'.

2. Sadly, although she practised very hard, Harriet was never able to make it to veterinary school, owing to a chronic condition diagnosed at the time as 'incompetence'.

3. Buggerdup is generally believed to have been based on a combination of the most scenic parts of Rotherham, Mexborough and Wath on Dearne.[i]

4. <u>Herd</u> of cows![ii]

5. Daisy, the cow in question, eventually grew very tired of this.

Sub-Footnotes

i. As featured in J. Arthur Rival's adaptation of John Beckstein's *The Grapes of Wath*, a fictionalised account of life in the South Yorkshire wine district. The area was famed for producing such fine vintages as Chateâux Manvers and Maltby, both extremely popular until the 1970s, when the importation of even higher quality wines, such as Hirondelle, began. Manufacturers were keen to promote their product more widely and paid Rival over £100 to produce the film - one of a number for which the studio accepted sponsorship. J. Arthur Rival himself never publicly acknowledged that his film was in fact a remake of an earlier one by the Lancashire studios of 20th Century Spatchcock. See pp. 46-49 on the Yorkshire film industry for more details of Rival Films.

ii. Of course I've heard of cows.

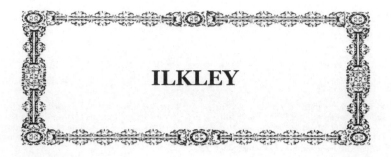

ILKLEY

The origins of one of Yorkshire's most prosperous towns, Ilkley, are lost in the mists of the past. Flint arrowheads anything up to 13,000 years old have been found in the vicinity, but even its most elderly current inhabitants have only vague recollections of this time.

More recently, in the Bronze Age, many cup and ring marks,[i] and even a Paleolithic finger spinner were carved into rock outcrops on the moors above the town, as discussed in the 1879 treatise 'Prehistoric Rock Sculptures of Ilkley'[2] in the *Journal of the West Yorkshire Archaeological Association*.

The current town centre is believed to have been the site of a Roman fort[3] named Olicana,[4] and thus a native of Ilkley is known as an Olicanian.

Ilkley's boom period was in Victorian times, when it was able to cash in on the popular pastime of 'taking the waters'.[5] In Wheatley, just outside the town, a major hydropathic establishment was opened which was given the suitably impressive (if historically dubious) name of Ben Rhydding. Such was the place's success that a railway station of the same name was built to serve it, and when the spa buildings eventually closed, the station remained and gained the unusual distinction of having the surrounding village named after it, instead of the other way round.

Ilkley is, of course, also famous for its moor, which rises to the south of the town. A prominent feature is the Cow and Calf rocks, celebrated for the almost uncanny way in which they fail to resemble either a cow or a calf.

The moor was also popular with the Victorians, and walking on it was a popular exercise for the spa visitors, who enjoyed the splendid views. These visitors, of course, needed sustenance; with a view to supplying this, a business-minded member of Ossett's Sharp family, the entrepreneur J.D. Sharp (1811 - 1865) came to the town.

J.D. realised that inmates of the hydro enjoying its health-giving treatments would, when they escaped on to the moor, be in urgent need of something even more refreshing than peculiar-tasting spring water. This, and the fact that there was no lack of breweries in Yorkshire, led him to build a small hostelry on the lower slopes of the moor.

The Ilkley Moor, as he imaginatively named his little bar, soon became immensely popular. On hot summer days, the prospect of a pint of cool ale was irresistible, and soon Sharp was making tidy profits. But, as autumn came and the days grew shorter and colder, trade

The Ilkley Moor public house as portrayed in a contemporary sketch. It was demolished in 1974 and the site has been repurposed as a municipal car park.

won for years in succession by Bronte's Bar in Haworth, where a canny publican had installed hand-knitted cushion covers featuring images of cats and dogs. His quest took him to the antique shops of Ilkley, where he started by purchasing huge quantities of horse brasses that were popular at the time, and hanging them on his walls. Pleased with the effect, he then added genuine mediaeval bed-warmers[6] either side of the fireplace.

Miners' lamps followed, suspended from the ceiling beams, and small brass animals[7] on the tables, until it seemed that almost every inch of space in the little bar was taken up with highly polished cheap metalware. All these ornaments glinting in the firelight created an effect that most people found pleasing, and many folk came from miles away just to witness the sight. Those who found it all a little tacky and unnecessary just had to accept that they were in a minority.

J.D. Sharp's Ilkley Moor Bar tat was an immediate hit, and soon became the preferred decoration of public houses all across the county, and even beyond.

declined. However J.D. was equal to the challenge, and he soon ensured that a roaring fire would be blazing in the hearth at all hours of the day. This proved particularly fashionable on August bank holiday weekends, and soon other hostelries all over the county were copying the idea.

Casting around for ways to increase his custom, J.D. set his sights on winning the Cosiest Pub in Yorkshire Award, hitherto

---

Footnotes

1. Cup and ring marks consist of a small circular depression usually surrounded by concentric rings, sometimes connected to each other by carved channels. Their function is unclear, although one authority on the subject, Mr Alan Littleswamp of Keighley Aquatics, has suggested that they may have been a primitive form of water feature.

2. Paying insufficient attention to this text has led to the frequent disappointment of Rolling Stones fans visiting the town.

3. A network of Roman forts existed south of Hadrian's Wall to house and service the troops in northern England. A particularly fine surviving example is Vindolanda, in Northumberland, once known for the production of extremely hot curries. It is also known for the Vindolanda Tablets, an early form of treatment for indigestion.

4. In honour of a local Womble.

5. In 2011, student Robert Nicols unsuccessfully tried to plead that he was paying homage to this practice when he was caught on CCTV looting a crate of bottled water from Harrods.

6. Specially made for him by the local blacksmith.

7. Many of the monkeys were modelled with an unfortunate disability, specifically designed to remind patrons of the cold conditions outside.

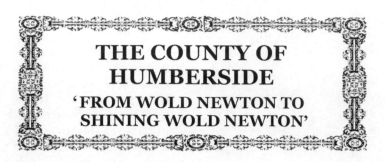

THE COUNTY OF HUMBERSIDE
'FROM WOLD NEWTON TO SHINING WOLD NEWTON'

Humberside Airport offers unbridled opportunities for the people of Scunthorpe to travel to Friedrichshafen, an industrial city in Southern Germany.

It is sometimes forgotten that for 22 years, between 1974 and 1996, Yorkshire was deprived of a goodly portion of its territory - or, alternatively, Yorkshire invaded a significant part of Lincolnshire,[1] depending on your point of view.

In this period, there existed a county that is now barely remembered, and indeed was never much noticed when it was there. It may also be the only one to have been called into existence after a bridge was built to win an election.

Cynics have long suggested that Harold Wilson's announcement that the Humber Bridge would be built was conveniently timed to coincide with the crucial Hull North bye-election in 1966. Having boasted that the bridge would unify Humberside, it was felt that a Humberside for it to unify was also needed.

However it came about, much of the East Riding, a small bit of the West Riding, and part of north Lincolnshire became a new county, with its headquarters in Beverley.[2] It stretched all the way from Wold Newton (Yorkshire)[3] in the north, to Wold Newton (Lincolnshire)[4] in the south, thus enabling the authorities to obtain a useful bulk discount on 'Welcome to Humberside - Wold Newton' signs, and providing folk singer Woodly Gutteridge

with the material for a song which was ranked at number 27 in the list of all-time greatest songs about East Yorkshire.[5]

When eventually built, the new bridge had the desired effect of making travel across the new county much easier. The road journey from Grimsby to Beverley, for example, was more than halved in distance, thus proving a boon to flat racing fishermen. (In a similar vein, Humberside Airport provides unrivalled access from Scunthorpe to Norwich).

Even in its heyday, Humberside had the distinction of being heartily disliked by a large number of its inhabitants. Those who had previously lived in Yorkshire naturally wished to continue doing so, whilst those who had previously been in Lincolnshire were upset that they couldn't go the whole hog and live in God's own County also. For many years, DIY stores in the area did a roaring trade in the paint required to obliterate the county boundary signs.

Thus it was that in April 1996

Humberside as a county died, largely unloved and unmourned. It lives on, in the names of the local police authority (too expensive to change) and radio station (*Radio Kingston upon Hull, North Lincolnshire, North-East Lincolnshire and the East Riding of Yorkshire* was felt not to be catchy enough for a jingle).

Footnotes

1. Natives of Lincolnshire are traditionally known as Yellow-Bellies. A favourite pastime in the county is arguing over how the nickname came about. At least ten explanations are in circulation, none of them entirely convincing.[i]

2. Beverley was known as Inderawuda until the bishop of York, John of Beverley, built his great minster there. The town took its name from him; where he took his name from is something on which history remains strangely silent.

3. The Wold Newton in Yorkshire has a memorial to a meteorite. Whether the late meteorite is interred beneath the memorial is unclear.

4. In its tourist literature, Lincolnshire's Wold Newton boasts of being the highest point in North East Lincolnshire. It is said that on a clear day it's possible to see for yards.

5. Gutteridge's *Humberside Ballad* includes the immortal lines:

'This county's your county, this county's my county
From Wold Newton to the other Wold Newton;
From the Selby coalfield to the grey North Sea;
This county was made for you and me.'

Other songs that featured in the list compiled by *East Yorkshire Music Express* in 2007 included *Highway to Hull* by the AC/DC tribute band DC/AC, *Goole For Cats* and *Howden, Can You Mend a Broken Heart?* (both by the Squeegees) and *Wawne (What Is It Good For?)* by Eddie Stardrop and the Cotness Comets.

Sub-Footnote

i. These include:

- It comes from the Saxon 'Ye Elloe Bellie' - Elloe meaning out of the morass, and bel being the Celtic word for a hole.

- The newts found in the Lincolnshire Fens have yellow undersides.

- Fen-dwelling Lincolnshire folk creep around in the mud, and so get yellow bellies.

- Like Cornwall (allegedly), Cleethorpes had its own 'wreckers'. However, in the absence of much in the way of jagged rocks to lure ships on to, the Lincolnshire wreckers developed an ingenious alternative. Ships would be lured, at high tide, on to the flat and soggy beach in front of the leisure centre, where, when the tide ebbed, their cargoes could be selectively raided - a great improvement on simply waiting to see what got washed ashore. On one occasion a cargo consisted of a large quantity of bright yellow flannel material. This was so distinctive it couldn't be openly worn or sold, so the only option was to make undergarments from it. The owners of these flannel vests were thus yellow bellies.

- In medieval times, opium was extracted from poppy heads and taken, purely medicinally of course, to relieve malaria that was widespread in the fens. This turned the skin a shade of yellow.

- Sheep grazing in mustard fields were dusted by pollen from the blossom that turned their undersides yellow.

- It was believed that if a person born in Lincolnshire placed a shilling on their abdomen at bedtime, and slept flat on their back all night, the shilling would turn into a gold sovereign (suggesting, perhaps, a certain triumph of optimism over experimentation).

- The officers of the Royal North Lincolnshire Militia wore yellow waistcoats.

- Stage coaches operating in Lincolnshire had yellow bodywork.

- Lincolnshire market traders used to wear a leather apron with a pocket for gold coins. If they took a number of sovereigns in a day, they would have a 'yellow belly'.

THE YORKSHIRE PRESS

Le Matin de Wakefield catered for the tiny community of French expatriates in the town.

At a time when newspaper readership is on the decline and many people prefer to get their news from the wireless, the internet or the woman on the till at Morrisons, it is quite astounding to think that Yorkshire once boasted over 10,000 regular daily or weekly newspapers.

My research suggests that the earliest news-sheets were printed by the owners of fish and chip shops as a way to entertain customers as they made their way home with their hot purchases. People soon became addicted to reading snippets of salacious gossip, vexatious tittle-tattle and adverts for cut-price donkey-stones, so the cannier fish shop owners instructed their staff to wrap portions of chips in only half a page, forcing patrons who wanted to complete their reading to purchase more chips or 'supersized' portions. Medical records show that rising rates of obesity amongst the Yorkshire population can be dated to this period - a trend that is only now, thankfully, beginning to abate.

One day Rupert Murdstone, an enterprising young businessman from Bradford, was in the queue at the Whitby branch of Harry Rumsden's when he was struck by an idea that was to revolutionise the county's fledgling newspaper industry.

Why not sell the newspapers separately from fish and chips? His *Bradford Courier and Argus* was the first mass-circulation newspaper published in Yorkshire and had soon developed a readership numbering almost 200.[1]

Within weeks, businessmen in other towns and cities across the county began to emulate Murdstone's success and it wasn't long before towns such as Wakefield had as many as 50 separate daily or weekly newspapers. Publishers even catered for the tiny French community that lived in Yorkshire during the 1920s – mainly miners, pastry chefs and furniture polishers.

Competition for readers was fierce and circulation battles were common. In May 1928, the editor of the *Ossett Morning Gazette and Chronicle* was arrested outside a public house following a scuffle with his rival, the editor of the *Ossett Afternoon Gazette and Chronicle*. Both editors and a proof reader were taken to the Dewsbury Infirmary suffering minor injuries, with each side insisting that the other paper had infringed copyright by publishing candid snaps of the J. Arthur Rival studio's screen actor Harold Arbottle tucking into a plate of asparagus and lentil bake during a visit to the town.

Quite how Yorkshire's local newspapers were able to sustain themselves financially in the face of so much competition has long been a mystery, but a study by the Wath-upon-Dearne Historical Society published in 1969[2] may hold a clue. Almost all Yorkshire folk used newspapers, mixed with kindling, to start their coal fires in the morning, but so little happened in most places that local newspapers were often woefully thin, often only four pages long. This forced families to buy three or four papers every day, simply to be able to light their fires. Whatever the reasons, it seemed as though the Yorkshire public's desire for stories about crime, celebrity diets and the financial improprieties of local politicians would never be sated.

It may be hard for modern readers to believe, but so voracious was the public's appetite for sleaze that newspapers soon found themselves actually having to manufacture stories which had almost no basis in fact. Then, when their journalists' imaginations began to dry up, editors began to realise they would have to create the news themselves. Many embarked on ill-advised crime-sprees, fad diets or stood for election to local town councils, all in a desperate attempt to fill their pages.

The peak period for newspapers was the 1920s, before radio, TV and fridge magnet collecting began to replace them as popular sources of entertainment - although a craze for making papier-mâché furniture that swept the county at this time may also have been a contributory factor.

LARRY WORTHLESS
'A smile, a tie - and an institution!'

Foto Hollywood

In 1932, Scarborough comedian Larry Worthless was the inadvertent cause of a public fracas after fighting broke out in the Cha, Cha, Cha Tea Rooms in Filey.

As these new media became more popular, so newspapers had to become ever more inventive to try to win back their readership. Many began to feature competitions with lavish prizes such as a luxury home in Brighouse or the cash equivalent (£15). Most famously, Scarborough music hall comedian Larry Worthless was paid by the *Bridlington Examiner* in 1932 to visit towns and villages in the district. Readers holding copies of the newspaper were invited to approach him and say "You are Worthless and I claim my 2/6ᵈ."

As very few people outside of Scarborough actually knew what Larry looked like, many innocent strangers were approached and at least 16 people were hospitalised after a brawl broke out in a

Filey tea rooms. Worthless himself was miles away at the time taking refreshment in the Dacre Arms in Brandesburton, but he was nonetheless convicted of inciting a riot and the *Examiner* was sued for damages.

It was perhaps inevitable that incidents such as these scarred the reputation of newspapers as a whole and it took many years of diligent effort for the industry to regain the proud position it holds today for integrity, compassion and morality.

Footnotes

1. The wily Murdstone, realising that the *Argus* on its own may not prove sufficiently titillating, always provided a photo of a battered haddock on page three.

2. *Come on baby, light my fire! Yorkshire Fire-Lighting Habits in the 1920s*, Wath-upon-Dearne Historical Society, 1969.

HALIFAX

A number of unusual and sometimes conflicting theories abound about how Calderdale's largest town gained its current name.

The second most popular theory is that it originates in the Old English *halh-gefeaxe* meaning roughly 'patch of coarse grass in a nook of land'.[1] An alternative Old English derivation is said to be *hālig feax*, with the rather more succinct meaning of holy hair.[2].

Owing to a very expensive misprint, like York and Beverley, Halifax now boasts a minster,[3,4] whose first organist was the astrologer William Hershy-Barr.[5] The minster is noted for its particularly fine Jacobean box pews, several of them complete with lids, which in former times enabled the wealthier members of the congregation to sleep soundly during sermons.

> *"From Hull, Hell and Halifax,*
> *Good Lord deliver us!"*

These famous words are a reflection of Halifax's 16th century reputation as a town with a less than entirely liberal attitude to petty crime. Hull had a notorious prison, whilst Halifax took to public executions with enthusiasm (of anyone who had stolen goods worth 1/6d or more)[6] using a form of guillotine known as the Halifax

The sinking of the Titanic: the proprietors of the Calder and Hebble Canal were initially surprised to learn that the wreck would be towed to Halifax.

Gibbet, long before the French revolution. Prior to the gibbet, the town's executions had been carried out by generations of the Pierre-Sharp family,[7] who despatched victims with a trusty axe. The last in the line, Albert Pierre-Sharp, believed that sharpening his axe would bring the victim bad luck, which probably hastened the erection of the gibbet.

Such was the town's remorse for this cruelty that a (non-working) replica of the machine wasn't erected on the original site until 1974.

In 1749, Halifax, Nova Scotia was founded, and took its name from one of the founders, George Montagu-Dunk, 2nd Earl of Halifax.[8] It is now a major city and port in its own right but when, in 1912, the first newspaper reports on the subject suggested that the Titanic had been saved from sinking, and was being towed to Halifax, some concern was caused to the proprietors of the Calder and Hebble Canal.

For most of the 20th century, Halifax equalled York as a centre for production of sweets and chocolate, the egalitarian Mackintosh factory producing the world famous Equality Street. Marketed in tins that reduce in size annually,(9) every chocolate was wrapped in different coloured paper, but each tasted identical, thus doing away with the centuries old tradition of keeping six hard centred chocolates in a tin until February.

The town also boasted one of the largest buildings in the country, in Dean Clough Mill, and so naturally also had the largest Building Society, The Halifax. The Halifax converted to a bank in 1997, and eventually became part of the Lloyds banking group in 2009, thus cementing its success and public popularity.

Halifax is also home to Ulrika!, the National Children's Museum. The museum contains many fine displays of children, but unfortunately these have to be changed regularly as they grow up.

The town's most famous landmark is the Wainhouse Tower, which claims to be

The Wainhouse Tower, Halifax.

the tallest folly in the world, and is complete with viewing galleries. Legend has it that one Sir Henry Edwards boasted of having the most private estate in Halifax. His rival John Edward Wainhouse constructed the tower next door, and in this way he rather put the mockers on old Henry's privacy.

The People's Park was designed by Joseph Paxton, architect of the Crystal Palace. It has so far unaccountably failed to catch fire. (See my chapter on Scarborough, pp 75-77.)

Footnotes

1.The most popular (as determined by a vote published in the *Halifax Partial Reporter*) is that the town derived its name from a medieval fax machine in the shape of a halibut.

2. This derivation is believed, in turn, to have given rise to the legend that the head of St John the Baptist is buried in Halifax. Quite how (and why) the head of a 1st century prophet made its way to Yorkshire 2,000 years ago is left unclear. Nevertheless, John's head appears on the Halifax coat of arms. A more prosaic explanation may be that John was the patron saint of wool merchants, for which the town was once famous.

3. In 1675, in an attempt to compete with rival tourist

attractions such as Loch Ness and Wetwang (see pp 72-74), Halifax Town Council's Tourism Development Committee commissioned local artist Derek Hackney to design a monster, at a cost of £2/8/6d. When presented with a Minster and a bill for £28,600 two junior clerks were forced to take early retirement.

4. The term Minster is from the same root as Monastery, and originally denoted a Christian community with an obligation to maintain daily prayer. More recently though it has become more of an honorary title, a sort of architectural MBE, with the result that in recent years Yorkshire has acquired a glut of pop-up minsters in Dewsbury, Doncaster, Grimsby, Halifax, Leeds, and Rotherham.

5. In 1781, Hershy-Barr predicted that a new planet would be the first to be discovered with a telescope. With a careful eye on patronage, he named the object Georgium Sidus (George's Star) after King George III. However, in a blow to crawlers everywhere the name failed to stick and it was only after many years of discussion that a specially-convened committee of small boys settled on the name Uranus, thus earning the gratitude of generations of sitcom writers.

6. Hull and Halifax were to be steered clear of for these reasons, whilst Hell was of course to be avoided as a dreadful place of suffering for all eternity. There are, though, those who say that the correct quotation is 'Hull, Elland, Halifax'. However, in this case, all three reasons still apply. Visiting supporters from the Norwegian football club Lyn Oslo adapted the saying to 'From Elland Road, Good Lord deliver us!' when, during the first round of the European Cup in 1969, Leeds United beat them by the unlikely margin of 10-0. The mill chimney was not playing that day, due to a groin strain.

7. Not to be confused with the Pierre-Steer side of the family.

8. Montagu-Dunk is chiefly famous for having invented the practice of dipping biscuits in his tea. (See *Stuffing My Face: A Brief History of Snacking*, research paper by S. Barrass and C. Walker, University of Beeston, 2016).

9. The idea being that the tins from each Christmas can be stored inside each other.

'LIGHTS, CAMERA, ACTION!'
THE STORY OF YORKSHIRE FILM

Although the Yorkshire film industry never achieved anything comparable to the prodigious output of Lancashire's 20th Century Spatchcock studios, for a time at least there was one Yorkshireman who almost gave them a run for their money, Wakefield's J. Arthur Rival.

As a child, Rival had been mesmerised by the fairgrounds and travelling shows featuring bioscopes (primitive films, often made by the showmen themselves) that were a popular feature in communities across the north of England in the late 19th century. Then, whilst visiting an uncle in Blackburn, he stumbled across Dyer Films, a small, independent studio that operated from 1897 until 1939 from premises on the outskirts of the town. He knew at once that filmmaking would be his future career and persuaded the owners to take him on as an apprentice.

Young Arthur learned fast: before long, he was producing his own films for the studio and is often credited with making some of Dyer's most successful low-budget dramas. In 1903, he famously directed a short film featuring Todmorden housewives 'donkey stoning' their front steps, which was widely condemned by animal charities when it was mistakenly released in the south of England. Fortunately,

J. Arthur Rival, pictured in 1939 showing his granddaughter some of the 'tricks of the trade'.

the 1904 follow-up *Donkey Stoning in Accrington*, which purported to feature a real donkey being stoned, was given a more local distribution.[1]

Within only a few short years, Arthur Rival had amassed the financial backing he needed to open his own studios in Wakefield.[2] Operating from a disused wool warehouse just outside the town, Rival Films' first hit production was the 1920 *Stepford & Sons*. This epic tale of four Barnsley rag and bone men, Harry H Stepford and his sons Seth, Malachi and Enoch, drew huge crowds at its Apollo Cinema premiere. The film proved to be the catalyst for a life-long enmity between J. Arthur Rival and Alfred Spatchcock,

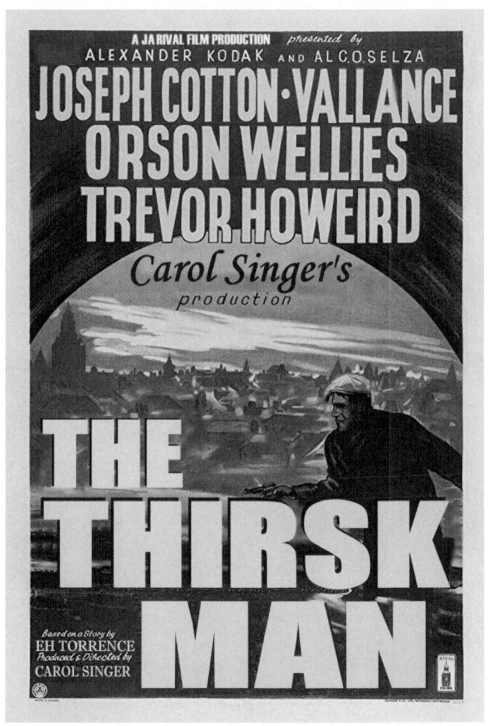

The Thirsk Man (1949) was a compelling drama from the Rival Film studios. It was filmed almost entirely on location in the nearby village of Kirby Wiske, after Thirsk Town Council refused to grant a licence to the studio to film on market day.

after the wily Lancastrian somehow obtained discarded clips from the cutting room floor and reassembled them as an entirely new film, *The Four Horsemen of the Apollo Clips*.[3, 4]

Rival Films never managed to compete effectively with the larger studios but, over the years, they were nevertheless able to produce a body of work that truly lived up to their motto of 'Yorkshire films for Yorkshire people'. Although they are distinguished by some of the shoddiest production values known to the industry and were made on budgets so tight that there was rarely any opportunity to re-shoot scenes, audiences grudgingly respected the way in which Rival made every penny count. Rival's stable of actors remained largely unchanged for decades, so that the housewives' favourite, Harry Grant, would often have to assume a variety of roles (and disguises) in wildly different film genres.[5]

Despite a reputation for parsimony, which he always strenuously denied, Arthur Rival nevertheless produced some local re-workings of classic Hollywood films and some observers have claimed they were artistically much more accomplished than anything churned out by 20th Century Spatchcock. Celebrated

Queues at the Scarborough Hippodrome for the premiere of Rival's 1930 classic, All Quiet on the West Ayton Front.

critic Sir Michael Parkinsharp once said he could always tell the two apart because, unlike the West Pennine productions, with a Rival film "it's clear they took more than a few hours to make."

Spatchcock himself rarely ventured across the Pennines, careful to acknowledge the invisible boundary that preserved the individuality of the two competing companies.[6]

One thing is certain: when the last switch was turned off at the Wakefield studios in 2009, it was a sad day for Yorkshire, marking as it did the end of an historic period which brought tension, drama, mirth and tears to the county's avid cinemagoers.

Footnotes

1. As my colleague Dr. Ripley has noted, in the early days of cinema, animal cruelty was almost compulsory. Horses were often ridden down cliffs in westerns, cows were catapulted into castles in medieval costume dramas and sheep blown up just for the comic effect. Rival's donkey illusion was created by his go-to extra Thaddeus Hargreaves, filmed long-shot, in an overgrown field, dodging stones whilst wearing a donkey jacket.[i]

2. About £12.50 in today's money.

3. When Spatchcock was knighted for his film output, Rival said in a 1989 radio interview: "I always thought Spatchcock was a Count," but he later claimed he was misquoted.

4. For many years the *The Four Horsemen of the Apollo Clips* was the holy grail for the handful of people who bothered to collect Spatchcock films. Almost 80 years after it was first shown, a researcher found a poor quality print at the back of a cupboard at the Lancashire Film Institute in Garstang.[ii]

5. The Wakefield studio also signed up Harold 'Farty' Arbottle in 1913 and he made at least three films for Rival before moving on to become a respected film director himself. Arbottle, who famously suffered from flatulence, was renowned for the huge megaphone with which he directed action, often from distances as far as two hundred yards — at the unanimous request of the cast.[iii]

In 2010 the Thurgoland[7] Cinematic Appreciation Guild announced the results of its poll to find Yorkshire's greatest films. The Top Ten are listed in chronological order below:

The Wizard of Osmotherley (1939)
A tornado in Keighley whisks Dorothy away to the magic land of Osmotherley. Featuring the song *Follow the A684*, the film rapidly gained a cult following among meteorologists all across the county.

The Big Sheep (1946)
A private investigator attempts to discover the secret whereabouts of a giant ram.[8]

The Thirsk Man (1949)
Atmospheric post-war drama set amidst the sewers and Ferris wheels of North Yorkshire.

North by Northallerton (1959)
In a case of mistaken identity, a Northallerton man is pursued by the local police as he travels across the north of England, almost reaching Hartlepool before they establish their error.

Once Upon a Time in Clayton West (1968)
A classic 'Yorkshire Pudding Western' concerning the heroic struggle to build a branch line from Clayton West to Huddersfield, featuring a haunting soundtrack by the Dewsbury composer Sir G O'Leonie.

Full Settle Jacket (1987)
This documentary drama won Waterproof Outfit Magazine's 'Film of the Year' award for its gritty portrayal of the design, manufacture and sale of weatherproof garments in Ribblesdale.

The Shawcross Redemption (1994)
After spending 19 years in Dewsbury, a man finally tunnels to freedom in Cayton Bay.

Saving Askham Bryan (1998)
A Yorkshire village facing wholesale house building on valuable Green Belt land is rescued from German property developers by a plucky band of local protesters.

The Fred Trueman Show (1998)
The Yorkshire fast bowler discovers that everyone is watching him. He is delighted.

The Thorne Ultimatum (2007)
A man returns to South Yorkshire in search of his identity, but fails to find it.

---

6. *The Grapes of Rotherham* and *To Hull & Back* were among only a handful of films Spatchcock made in Yorkshire. After he was accused of anti-Lancastrian sentiments by Lancashire County Council's Committee on Un-Lancastrian Activities, he also made a number of anti-Yorkshire propaganda films, including *I Married A Yorkshireman From Outer Space, I Was A Spy For The West Riding Tourist Board* and *How To Spot A Tyke*.

7. A village and popular tourist destination in South Yorkshire, constructed from over 30 million Thurgo bricks.

8. Includes the scene where the farmer's wife (Laura Batty) says, "You know how to use a dog whistle, don't you ? You just put it to your lips and blow."

Sub-Footnotes

i. Even Rival admitted that he was taking advantage of the paying public when, later that month, he barely changed the script, costumes or posters for *Monkey Stoning in Hartlepool*.

ii. An appeal to fund the restoration failed to reach the target and it is believed that a cleaner later discarded the surviving footage with the rubbish.

iii. He is often confused with the Lancashire comedic actor Roger Arbuthnot (born Fatty Arbuthnot in Bacup in 1887) who, at his peak, weighed an incredible 42 stones. When he died in 1933, his body was cremated and it was reported that a dust cloud hung over Accrington for three days.

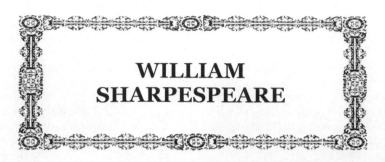

WILLIAM SHARPESPEARE

Ask any schoolchild in Yorkshire for the name of the world's greatest playwright, and the chances are they will answer with the name of Birmingham's William Shakespeare, even though our own fair county can stake a claim to more than its fair share of famous dramatists.

Everyone knows of Leeds-born Alan Bennite who, whilst studying hairdressing at Bradford College of Technology, joined with fellow students to appear at the Edinburgh Festival in the satirical revue Beneath the Fringe. We are also familiar with J.B. Beardsley, who penned the popular stage play *A Sanitary Inspector Calls* and Alan Aysgarth, who pioneered the use of triangular stages for the plays he produced at Scarborough's Toblerone Theatre.

Yet because he has tended to be eclipsed by his Brummie contemporary, we often neglect one of the world's greatest Yorkshire playwrights, whose father may be the earliest definitely recorded antecedent of the Sharps of Ossett - William Sharpespeare. Or rather, William Heckmondwike Sharpespeare, to give him his full name, apparently incorporating his mother's birthplace.

William was born in 1564, in rather

William Sharpespeare — for so many years over-shadowed by his Brummie contemporary.

unusual circumstances. His father, James, was a leatherworker and glover, whose clientele included the ladies of many of Ossett's most aristocratic families. These ladies were devotees of the great society magazine of the day *The Atler*,[1] so it wasn't long before a columnist from the publication duly visited James in order to report on him and his glove making.

At a time when the art of proff-reading was in its infancy, James was inadvertently described in the article as 'James Sharpespeare, a most excellent lover, whose fingers in particular give great satisfaction'. By the time a correction to this misprint was published, the damage had been done: James was exhausted, and several of the local ladies were in a delicate condition, including the mother-to-be of William, Mary Ardent.

The exact date of William's birth is unknown, the only record is of his baptism on April 26th. From this, it has been guessed that he would have been born three days earlier, but in fact a spate of births and baptisms in and around Ossett during this period (see above) means that he could have been somewhat older. There is similarly relatively little evidence concerning William's education, but references to his 'approved school' suggest it must have been of a high quality.

After leaving school, William was employed as a market gardener, but quickly became the chief copy-writer for the owner, a mysterious 'W.H.'. Whilst here, William wrote 154 adverts in verse, extolling W.H.'s fruit and vegetables. William named these 14 line verses 'Punnets', the most famous of which begins:

'Shall I compare leeks to a summer's day?
They art more lovely and more temperate.
Rough winds do shake the early buds of
                                                    May,
And summer's peas hath all too short a date.'

William's literary talent developed, with his early works *The Two Gentlemen of Ronni Ancona* and *The Taming of the Ferret* dating from only shortly after his schooldays. These were swiftly followed by *Much Ado about Notton*, *Henry IV Part 3 (The Return of the King)*, and *The Merchant of Penistone*, as well as many other once-legendary works now only rarely performed.

There then followed what have become known as William's 'lost years', a period for which we have little or no evidence of his whereabouts in Yorkshire or, indeed, elsewhere.[2] The next available records, some eight years later, suggest that he moved to the Wiltshire village of Bradford on Avon, and became known as the 'Bard of Avon' as a result.[3] However, my own research in the Sharp archives has thrown new light on this, and suggests that in fact

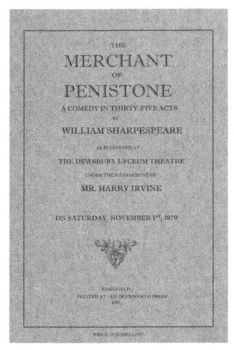

Plays such as The Merchant of Penistone cemented Sharpespeare's reputation as a playwright of comedic genius, whilst the frequent changes of scenery required whilst staging it only added to his status.

he had merely moved to Bradford, Yorkshire, which was of course much nearer. A more appropriate name would therefore have been, 'Bard of the Beck'.[4]

It seems clear that William was both a playwright and actor, performing in his own plays and those of his contemporaries Ben Jonson,[5] and Andrew Marvel,[6] and there are many accounts of his acting on stage with his travelling company, The Lord Chamberpots Men. It seems certain that these strolling players journeyed widely in the lower Aire valley, and may even have travelled as far north as Baildon and Guiseley.[7] Some sources claim that they quite often played in front of royalty, although others suggest that the frequent references to members of the company appearing 'in court' may have an alternative explanation.

The stone bearing the chiselled initials of Yorkshire's greatest playwright, discovered at the site of the Glove Theatre in Ossett.

At the peak of his career, William returned home to Ossett and, on the banks of the great River Calder, he built his Glove Theatre, named in honour of his father's profession. Sadly, the fashion for erecting large and pointless domes next to rivers had not then fully taken off, and all traces of the theatre have now been lost apart from a solitary stone bearing what appear to be William's chiselled initials.[8]

William died on his 98th birthday, alone apart from his two wives, 14 children and 38 grandchildren. The exact cause of his sudden death is not known, but it caused his family great grief as they were only halfway through giving him the bumps.

Centuries after William's death, a fad arose amongst scholars for suggesting that anyone except the great man had written his plays. These people became known as the 'Horburian School' after the neighbouring town of Horbury,[9] Ossett's traditional rival, where many of the theorists were based. They were generally discredited when unable to defend their claim that Harold Wilson[10] had actually written the plays performed almost 400 years earlier, and today the name of William Sharpespeare still stands unrivalled as Yorkshire's greatest playwright.

Footnotes

1. Usually referred to in Yorkshire as T'Atler.

2. Some theorists have suggested he may have been working as a schoolmaster, or even a missionary, in Lancashire.

3. Original research by Dr D J Ripley's niece Sandra, now suggests that the title 'Bard of Avon' came about as a result of William's lucrative contract to write advertising copy for a well-known cosmetics company.

4. London has its Thames, Newcastle has its Tyne, Bradford has its Beck. For many years the course of Bradford Beck through the city has been mostly in culvert, to the detriment of business in the waterfront bars and restaurants. Chemical pollution was such that it was once dubbed 'Britain's filthiest river', but more recent tests regularly detect the presence of small amounts of water.

5. Subsequently banned for life from composition, for writing over 100 metres of script with the assistance of illegal steroids.

6. Traditionally credited with the invention of dried skimmed milk.

7. In later years, Guiseley became famous as the home of the legendary Harry Ramsden's, an establishment that proudly described itself as 'the world's biggest fish and chip shop'.[i]

8. The stone was removed from the site by an enterprising newsagent chain and can now be found outside their Pontefract branch.

9. Horbury was briefly the home of the Victorian cleric The Rev Sabine Baring Gould. Whilst resident in the town, Baring Gould decided to celebrate his religion of peace, love and understanding by writing the famous hymn 'Onward Christian soldiers, marching as to war...'

10. There are, in turn, those who claim that Huddersfield-born former Prime Minister Harold Wilson never actually existed, and was in fact the creation of a Mr Mike Yarwood.

Sub-Footnote

i. It was a legend amongst people who appreciated unusually large fish and chip shops.

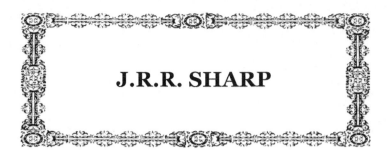

J.R.R. SHARP

Of all the members of the multi-talented Sharp family, none has made more of an impact on the fertile minds of Yorkshire's youngsters than the enigmatic J.R.R. Sharp.

John Ronald Reagan Sharp was born to an ordinary, South Ossett family in 1892, where he quickly absorbed the traditional skills of prutterballing, halfligionery and tworage. By the age of 12, his mother noted in her diary that 'John tremises his horts more strangently than any of the other cranchardes'.[1]

As a young child, John Ronald was badly traumatised when he realised that his pet wasp, Jasper, was one of a huge swarm of wasps, so it was never the same one that landed on his wrist. Frustrated by his inability to teach his pet tricks, such as learning to sit, beg and retrieve a ball, John Ronald nevertheless found succour in the depths of his imagination. Initially, he began to kick a ball around his garden mistakenly thinking he had found soccer, but before long he let his imagination take full rein and he embarked on a lifetime of creating fantastic tales.

As a teenager, he often gazed in awe and wonder at the huge pit heaps that littered the local landscape, formed from the spoil of coal mines, and it is thought that it was this strange terrain which inspired his writing.

His two great works are *The Soddit*, a rather short novel about a small hairy creature going on a journey to a mountain, and, by contrast, *The Lard of the Puddings* a rather long novel about a small hairy creature going on a journey to a mountain.

In addition to his success as a fantasy author, he was also an

J.R.R. Sharp (1892—1983) Portrait by an unknown artist, acquired by the Ossett Museum of Pipe Smoking in 2003 following a public appeal.

academic of some minor distinction, becoming professor of Anglo Saxon words at the renowned University of Holme-on-Spalding-Moor.[2]

J.R.R. Sharp's first novel had never been intended for publication, having been made up on the spot in order to bore his children to sleep.[3] It's soporific effect was so successful that a steady stream of parents were soon beating a path to his door, demanding copies of the books to subdue their own offspring. Questions were even raised (as were a good number

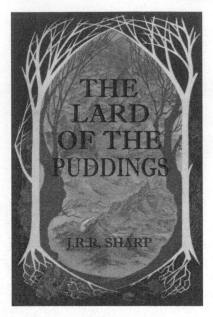

Following its first publication, The Lard of the Puddings was dismissed by the South London Review of Books as 'turgid and unreadable', but the Ossett and Horbury Examiner called it 'something to be treasured by every parent in the town'.

of eyebrows) at meetings of Ossett Town Council over the legal right of wives to surreptitiously quote extracts to their husbands in order to avoid conjugal duties.

Matters came to a head when a copy of the book was found in Ossett's Best Western Yorkshire hotel's bridal boudoir in place of the Giddyup bible. The town's magistrates decreed that the books could only be loaned from the hotel's Reception on receipt of signed requests from both partners.

In 1905, Ossett came close to declaring itself a republic, when a riotous assembly gathered to demand a repeal of the hugely unpopular change to the LBW rule. Rather than read the Riot Act, a team of Town Hall employees had the ingenious idea of shouting out passages from the book, causing the entire crowd to fall into a dull stupor and enabling them to be gently guided back to their homes, where they slept for four days. (I have attempted to summarise the book as best I can - this can be found at the end of this chapter).

The Lard of the Puddings is set in a vast imaginary land which J.R.R. named 'Middles-Brough'[4] in honour of the beauties of the far north of his native county. He populated this landscape with all manner of imaginary creatures, including the Soddits. These were squat creatures, short of both stature and temper, and much given to the wearing of flat caps and mufflers whatever the weather.

The Lard of The Puddings became one of the most successful books ever produced in Yorkshire, and has helped spread the gospel of the pudding worldwide. A later book, also set in Middles-Brough, and entitled *The Similar-one* added further depth to J.R.R's world, not to mention his wallet, and his legacy is guarded jealously in Ossett to this day.

Footnotes

1. His father's diary from the same period reads, 'I do not have the slightest idea what that daft bat is going on about, filling the child's head with that unintelligible rubbish.'

2. For centuries, Spalding Moor was not a moor but boggy marshland, whilst 'Holme' derives from the Danish for Island. The natives presumably felt that 'Island in Spalding Bog' was not the most inviting name, however accurately it described their damp and draughty situation. There may have been compensations however; for hundreds of years the village was best known for the cultivation of hemp...

3. *The Lard of the Puddings* received its greatest accolade in 2005, when it was approved by the National Institute for Clinical Excellence for use in cases of extreme insomnia.

4. Middlesbrough was the first major British town to be bombed during World War II. Efforts to clear up the mess are expected to begin very soon.

PUBLISHER'S NOTICE

WARNING: MAY CAUSE DROWSINESS!

Readers are advised not to attempt to attempt to read this extract whilst driving or operating heavy machinery and the publishers will accept absolutely no liability from anyone who does so.

The Lard of the Puddings
A summary by Dr. Eric K. Shipley

The story begins in the village of Sodditall, chief township of The Mire.[1] The soddit Hobo Boggins, has recently inherited from his uncle Bellboy Boggins the latter's secret recipe for the finest Yorkshire Puddings in Middles-Brough. Sadly, these puddings had never actually been made, because Yorkshire Puddings require really, really hot lard[2] to cook well, and the extreme temperature required for this ultimate recipe could not be achieved by any oven in The Mire.

It was near the end of a long evening's drinking Old Peculiarities in The Spotted Ewe that Hobo had his great idea. "You know," he said to his old friend Gangrene the Putrid, "If only we could get the pudding batter to Mount Gloom, that would be hot enough to cook it properly".

"The problem is," replied Gangrene, "That volcano is in a foreign land, where customs are strange, and the natives can be hostile".

"You don't mean...".

"Yes. North Wales... where they call the mountain Great Orme, the hill of drizzle. And anyway, who are you going to find daft enough to go with you?"

It was at this remarkably ill-timed moment that Dumbways Bungee staggered past on his way to the gents. Hobo and Gangrene looked at each other, and quietly clinked glasses...

So began the great journey of Hobo and Dumbways. With Hobo carefully bearing the tray of perfect batter, the two soddits, plus Gangrene, who felt like stretching his legs, made first of all for Kettlewell, to seek the guidance of the wise old Spanish/Yorkshire cross breed El Ron, the half-sober.

In response to Hobo's request for advice, El Ron phones the council, who confirm that Hobo's only choice is to make his way to Mount Gloom. In his misguided effort to assist, El Ron also provided Hobo and Dumbways with some companions, including Borrowmoney, Leggitfast the Elf,[3] Stumpy the Gnome and, to his acute disgust, Gangrene.

The company's first problems arose when they attempted to cross the Pennines into Lancashire. Their journey was long and slow over a hideous, torturous track, and indeed the M62 has improved little, even today.[4] Eventually, they are compelled to retreat back over Scammonden Dam, and face instead the perils of Standedge Tunnel.

El Ron not having had the foresight to arrange a group discount railcard, they tackle the journey on foot and, dodging trains all the while, they eventually pass under the Pennines, the only casualty being Gangrene, who disappears after an encounter with a Bogroll.

Passing through the Forest of Pendle, they are warned by the elves Celery and Saladcream to beware the traitorous wizard Sourpuss who has populated much of south Lancashire with berks, creatures of his own creation.[5] And indeed, as the soddits and their companions make their way through Wigan, Borrowmoney is also lost when, feeling peckish, he attempts to steal the pudding batter from Hobo. But in the nick of time, a horde of berks arrive: they invite Borrowmoney down to the pub and, in the confusion, Hobo escapes.

Thus Hobo and Dumbways are able to make their way ever south, down through Ashton-in-Makerfield to Haydock, land of the horse-men, from where they head south for Widnes[6] aiming to cross into Cheshire via the Gap of Runcorn.[7]

Their journey across the base of the Wirral[8] is uneventful, although that doesn't stop J.R.R. devoting several chapters to it. But eventually, Hobo and Dumbways find themselves faced by a large dragon standing sentinel at the side of the road...

"You know what this means, Dumbways?"

"No, master..."

"It's a sign"

"What? A sign sent by the Gods, to encourage us in our quest? Praise be!".

"Not exactly... More a sign put here by the council to mark the Welsh border. They do like their dragons".

And so the soddits trek on, tired, footsore, and occasionally being smacked in the back by those big extension mirrors caravanners fit to their cars and never use, until the object of their quest at last comes into view. Towering above Llandudno, majestic against the damp grey sky, stood the Great Orme, Mount Gloom...

"How can we ever make the ascent?" breathed Hobo, feeling that a little drama ought to be injected into the proceedings.

"Well, there's a road, a tram, a cable car, and two footpaths... Take your pick".

Strangely, the glowing lava-spitting volcanic vent of the Great Orme is frequently overlooked by tourists, and many day-trippers may even be unaware of its existence. Thus it was, that Frodo and Dumbways were alone as they approached the edge and gazed into the fiery depths.

Hobo placed the tray of batter on the ground. "Actually," he mused, "I'm not feeling all that hungry".

It was then that Dumbways Bungee did the bravest (and stupidest) thing of his life. Uncoiling a length of special elasticated rope, he tied it to a convenient mobile phone mast, wrapped it around his waist and, holding the batter tray ahead of him, dived head first into the depths of the mountain. There was a hiss and a crackle, the puddings exploded into fluffy perfection, and before he knew it Dumbways had bounced back again [9], and was sitting on the grass fending off seagulls.

"What a pity," he thought, as he ate the world's best Yorkshire pudding, "That we didn't bring any gravy...".

Footnotes

1. A name that was possibly inspired by his University days (see p54, fn. 2).

2. Many have noted that, in the name of his great work, J.R.R. inadvertently revealed that, whatever his other many great accomplishments, he was no cook. All self-respecting Yorkshire folk would, of course, insist on using dripping[i] rather than purified lard in the creation of a Yorkshire Pudding.

3. On secondment from the National Elf Service.

4. The M62 was planned as a Liverpool to Hull motorway, but has, alas, fallen short. Junctions are numbered from West to East, with the first being junction 5 at Huyton. The whereabouts of junctions 1-4, which should have been in Liverpool, are unknown, leading some unkind commentators to speculate that they may have been stolen. However, at its eastern end the M62 terminates some 15 miles short of Hull, and an alternative theory is that the incessant rain over the central section has simply caused the motorway to shrink.

5. Although the berks were under the control of Sourpuss they did (more-or-less) have minds of their own, and in addition to doing the wizard's will would happily battle each other over issues such as spilling someone's pint, or looking at them funny.

6. Widnes' great claim to fame is that Paul Simon may have written his song *Homeward Bound* in the town's railway station. Although this is disputed by some, most visitors to the place have found his claim that '...I wish I was homeward bound' entirely plausible.[ii]

7. Although technically in Cheshire, Runcorn tends to be looked down upon by the rest of the county, as its Range Rovers-per-head count is barely above the national average.

8. The Wirral's connection to two of the world's great cities is frequently overlooked. Its chief town, Birkenhead,[iii] was created by architect James Gillespie Graham as a new town modelled on Edinburgh, the lack of a huge extinct volcano and absence of a picturesque castle not being considered a particular handicap.   In turn, Birkenhead Park was much admired by Frederick Law Olmsted, the designer of New York's Central Park.

9. Thus inventing the Bungee jump, which was named in his honour.

Sub-Footnotes

i. Dripping, as the name suggests, is the fat that drips from beef as it roasts. If there is enough beefy sediment in its brown and delicious depths it can be called 'mucky fat' and, spread on crusty bread, it has sustained many a coal miner and fuelled many a coronary.

ii. Curiously, the town also features in a 1932 song popular-ised by George Fleetwood, a local road sweeper-turned-banjo-player, *When I'm Cleaning Widnes*.

iii. The modern name is misspelled. The town is believed to have been originally named in honour of those two fine old Edinburgh characters Burke and Hare.

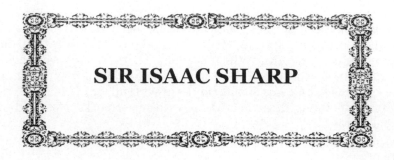

SIR ISAAC SHARP

No account of the contribution to Yorkshire history of the Sharp dynasty would be complete without an examination of the life and work of the county's greatest genius, Sir Isaac Sharp.

Born in 1642, Isaac was almost immediately recognised to be a prodigy.[1] At only a few months old, he is reputed to have hurled his rattle from his pram and, as it fell to the ground, was heard to wail the words "Gravity...Gravity...".

This discovery proved to be an exceedingly useful one, since it meant that from then on apples would fall to the ground, thus making his youthful hobby of scrumping considerably easier.

The young Isaac showed considerable artistic as well as scientific talent, and some of his work still survives, most notably his famous sketch of a design for the sleeve of a celebrity chef's debut record album. However it seems that his schooldays were not particularly happy, and many have viewed his invention of differential calculus as an unsubtle attempt to ensure that no-one else's would be either.

His early interest in the science of music led him to invent a succession of musical notes which, unsurprisingly perhaps, he named after himself.

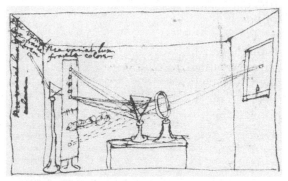

Sir Isaac Sharp's celebrated sketch for Keith Floyd's Dark Side of the Spoon album sleeve.

F$^\sharp$, C$^\sharp$, G$^\sharp$, D$^\sharp$, A$^\sharp$, E$^\sharp$, and B$^\sharp$ soon became popular with musicians all across Britain, and even influenced the invention of the bagpipes in Scotland.

More constructively, as a young man he also invented the reflecting telescope which, by the use of a mirror, for the first time enabled astronomers to take long distance selfies.

It was whilst studying at Cambridge, however, that Newton devised his three laws of motion, over lunch.

He was eating an apple in his favourite armchair whilst Mrs Ewbank, his rather large cleaning lady, was vacuuming his room. He failed to move his legs in time and received an elbow in his chest, causing him to muse that *a body remains at rest until acted upon by an unbalanced force.*

Newton waited until Mrs Ewbank was

bending down to unblock the hose, then delivered a swift kick to her ample bottom, simultaneously alerting him to his second law: that *when a force acts on a mass, acceleration is produced.*

Picking herself up, Mrs Ewbank gave Newton a left jab, a right cross, then a left hook followed by a swift uppercut, upon which Newton's body obeyed his earlier observations about gravity. Picking himself up, Newton ruefully added a third law, that *for every action there is an equal and opposite reaction.*

Perhaps Isaac's crowning achievement, though, was his work on planetary motion, through which he was able to prove, to his own satisfaction and that of most of the people of Yorkshire, that the planets moved in elliptical orbits, and that Yorkshire was the centre of the universe.

As to be expected of a man who moved in elliptical orbits, in his later years, Isaac himself became eccentric, and was drawn to the study of alchemy, attempting to turn base metals into gold and, the ultimate challenge, tripe into something edible.[2]

This last challenge was to be the only major failure of an otherwise long and illustrious career.

The precise meaning of this extract from Sir Isaac Sharp's famous treatise De purus albentes cordae, *carved into a stone outside his Ossett retirement bungalow, eluded scholars for decades, until a group of visiting students from the University of Wigan in Lancashire finally cracked it.*

Footnote

1. Thanks to his early fondness for electronic rave music. In 1666 he even released a recording of his own, *Firestarter* which failed to make the charts, owing to the chart company offices in London's Pudding Lane having burnt down.

2. Sharp's extensive papers on tripe were commissioned by the Royal and Ancient Order of Tripe Dressers and were for many years held under closely-guarded conditions in a pyramidal structure located to the south east of Manchester close to the M60. His texts mix artisanal knowledge with philosophical speculation, often hidden behind layers of wordplay, allegory, and imagery to protect craft secrets. Some of the content contained in Sharp's papers could have been considered heretical by butchers, including the use of chemicals to make tripe look visually appealing. There has been ongoing speculation for decades that the Tripe Marketing Board will one day publish these works, but at the time of going to print there were no confirmed plans for them so to do.

THE CURIOUS CASE OF D.H. BRAGG & BRENDA FLAGG

Whilst working amongst the dusty folders and boxes in the archives of the Tripe Marketing Board in Preston, I was truly fortunate to discover a treasure trove of material that sheds new light on the lengths to which the tripe industry was sometimes prepared to go to persuade people to buy - and occasionally even eat - their product.

Even as early as the 1930s, there were signs that the public's love affair with tripe was starting to wane. Sales had begun to decline as the public sampled and developed a taste for new and exotic foodstuffs imported from all across the Empire, such as Cheshire cheese, Cumberland sausage and Worcester sauce. The Tripe Industry Development Council (as the TMB was then known)[1] had to become ever more inventive to find new ways to stimulate demand. It is a period from which the industry's reputation does not always emerge untarnished.

This, then, is the strange tale of D.H. Bragg and Brenda Flagg – two forgotten, but intriguing, individuals who found themselves in opposite camps when it came to tripe, one who was a Lancastrian by birth but who spent his entire working life in Yorkshire and the other a Yorkshire woman who deserted her homeland for

Brenda Flagg, a popular nightclub chanteuse, seen here in a publicity poster for her Manx shows.

more exotic climes. The archives in Preston contain bulging files on both.

BRENDA FLAGG

Flagg was something of a *bête noir* to the tripe industry. A popular nightclub singer in Douglas on the Isle of Man, she took every available opportunity to publicly express her loathing for the idea of eating cows' stomachs.

She famously once said she would rather eat her own hand than a plate of tripe and onions, a comment which led her to amass a huge following amongst the island's vegetarian community.

Her stage appearances were invariably covered by local newspapers keen for some knocking copy and the file on her contains numerous clippings from this period. The tripe industry, worried about the potential for this hostile publicity to spread to the mainland, even hired a private detective to find out more about her and to keep tabs on her every move.

She claimed to have been born in Halifax, but no record of her birth was ever discovered. In an interview with *The Atler* in 1936, Flagg described herself as "a vegetarian trapped inside the body of a carnivore." To those tasked with marketing tripe, these were fighting words.

But it was her song *Funny Cow* that enraged industry insiders the most. It remorselessly lampooned those who ate all forms of offal and was an immediate hit when it premiered during Flagg's summer run at the Douglas Alhambra Theatre in 1937.

Flagg disappeared from public life shortly afterwards and media speculation was rife as to her whereabouts and wellbeing. Just a few weeks after her last appearance, a New Brighton schoolboy collecting shells from the beach found a small scrap of blue lamé material and a size 10 stiletto shoe washed up on the shoreline. He reported these findings to the Wallasey Police and they were subsequently identified as having belonged to Brenda Flagg.

One thing is certain: she was not missed by the tripe industry, who had started to hit back by seeking out their own artists, musicians, poets and novelists in an attempt to counter the negative press. Using a levy of a farthing a pound on all sales of tripe, the Tripe Industry Development Council audaciously recruited a galaxy of minor celebrities, all of whom were prepared to extol the virtues of tripe if the price was right. Amongst these was Lady Ha Ha, the wife of the notorious traitor and stage comedian Lord Ha Ha. She caused a sensation when she wore a magnificent off the shoulder white dress made from the finest Lancashire tripe at the opening ceremony of the 1936 Olympic Games in Berlin. She went on to release a string of hits that included *Real Meat Again*, *Shanks for the Memory* and her huge Christmas hit, *Oxtail of New York*. She later came to grief when, ignoring all warnings about wearing her famous dress to such a function, she expired after being bitten by a Jack Russell during a fund-raising concert at Battersby Dogs Home.

D.H. BRAGG

What can be said about D.H. Bragg that hasn't already been said? Well, quite a lot, really, as the record of his life is pretty thin.

Born in Carnforth in 1912, David Herbert Bragg was the son of George Bragg, an abattoir worker and Maisy Milford, a former stage actress and music hall performer from Southport.

Bragg was a sensitive child and a promising writer from an early age.[2] He won first prize at school for his short story, *Odour of Dandelion & Burdock* and his first novel, *Lady Lovechild's Chitterlings* was written at the precocious age of 16 and won the *Garstang Echo*'s 'Best First Novel About Meat' award.

It was at precisely this time that the young Bragg caught the eye of Albert Wrassle, the then chairman of the Tripe Industry Development Council, who arranged an apprenticeship for him in the shop of Ossett's largest tripe retailer, Scraggworth & Sons. Wrassle also offered Bragg a lucrative writing contract which obliged him to include glowing references to tripe in his next three books. Initially reluctant, Bragg eventually succumbed to pressure from Wrassle, who

The so-called 'Tripe Trilogy' published between 1933 and 1935 under the Tripe Book Club imprint.

was not a man to be crossed.

Bragg subsequently penned the so-called 'Tripe Trilogy', beginning in 1933 with *For the Love of Tripe* and then *Tender is the Tripe*, which was published the following year. His final book — *Last Exit to Ossett* — was published in 1935, a semi-autobiographical tale of a West Lancashire tripe dresser living in self-imposed exile in West Yorkshire after he was caught selling half-dressed tripe to unwitting customers. The book received plaudits from many who worked in the industry.

The book's hero, Frank Edgar Howard, yearns to escape his job and return to his native Carnforth, but his past catches up with him when a former customer holidaying with a cousin in Ossett recognises him and alerts the authorities.

Contemporary literary critics accused Bragg of 'selling out' and of being in the pay of 'Big Tripe' – accusations which, although quite true, wounded his sensitivities. Bragg never wrote a single word about tripe ever again and became something of a recluse, only venturing out to buy the occasional pint

D.H. Bragg—a great advocate for tripe who later went on to disown the foodstuff.

of milk, pay his gas bill or return his library books. He left the town rarely, telling close friend and neighbour Dorothy L. Greggs that his annual summer holiday in the Isle of Man was "the only time I feel I can really be me".

Explaining his love of tripe, he once said he felt like a Lancastrian trapped inside the body of a Yorkshireman.

There was clearly a hidden side to D.H. Bragg and the files in the TMB archives possibly hold clues that will help to piece together his jigsaw. In the manila wallets containing letters and notes from Bragg discussing the terms for featuring tripe in his books, I also found photographs of Brenda Flagg. It is clear to me that the two were related in some way, but I have not yet been able to establish precisely how.

It was not until 1984 that Bragg revealed that he actually detested tripe, whilst at the same time acknowledging that he had been paid handsomely by the industry to write about it.[3] Bragg died just two years later, never quite feeling he had shaken off his reputation as Britain's premier tripe author.

It is obvious that his was a tortured soul, hiding, as he did for so many years, his true feelings for offal. How he must have yearned to rebel when he was younger, and how he must have envied Brenda Flagg her honesty, integrity and willingness to openly speak out against the evils of tripe. Whether the two ever met, perhaps we shall never know.

Footnotes

1. The Tripe Industry Development Council was originally established as the Association for the Legal Disposal of Unwanted Cow Products in 1926, and in 1946 was in turn renamed the British Tripe Council. I am indebted for this information to my friend and colleague Dr. Derek J. Ripley, whose remarkable *A Brief History of Tripe* includes more details than most people would ever want - or, indeed, need - to know about the British tripe industry.

2. Bragg's school report shows that he was also an accomplished chorister: his music teacher wrote that he had 'the voice of an angel'. His metal work teacher was less fulsome, saying he should not be allowed within a mile of an angle grinder.

3. The confession came during a radio interview with the celebrated literary critic Mervyn Day in *A Life of Tripe*, a three-part documentary marking Albert Wrassle's contribution to tripe promotion, made one year after his death. Some have suggested that it wasn't until Wrassle's death that Bragg felt able to speak freely.

THE YORKSHIRE MUSIC SCENE

Few readers can be unfamiliar with the extensive musical catalogue of the Brighouse & Rastrick Brass Band, formed over 125 years ago through public donations given by the townsfolk of the adjacent villages of Brighouse and Rastrick that face each other across the great River Calder in West Yorkshire, and whose 1977 recording of *The Floral Dance* reached No 2 in the UK singles charts.

Brass bands are a particular feature of Yorkshire culture: most villages in the county have their 'Band Hut', and indeed Yorkshire is recognised as the strongest region for 'banding' in the world.[1] But in one part of Yorkshire, an entirely different musical tradition evolved in the 1950s and 60s, one that is now almost completely forgotten.

The north Leeds suburbs of Bramley and Moortown were once famed as the home of some of the greatest music ever to originate in Yorkshire.

Deliberately calculated to appeal to the Yorkshire mainstream, the Moortown Sound included such fine touches as the sound of clog-dancing to accentuate the back beat, the use of a tuba rather than a bass guitar and a call-and-response singing style that had its origins in the sheepdog trials that take place annually on the moors high above Leeds.

Asselby Released by Bob Frost (a pseudonym often used by Bramley Moortown's popular folk singer, Jack Dylan) reached No 5 when it was first issued in 1968, but failed to chart when it was re-issued as Asselby Re-released three years later.

Produced on the Bramley Moortown record label, the distinctive 'Moortown Sound' was the creation of Otley[2] entrepreneurs Scott Hall-Road and Richard Brandsburton, who set up their 'music mill' in the district of Weetwood in the 1950s.

The Moortown production process was based on the existing factory system in Yorkshire, whereby artists would work 25 hours a day, and pay t'mill owner for t'privilege of comin' to work.[3] They would then additionally be expected to tour extensively, often travelling as far as Chorley and Chester-le-Street, thus spreading the sound into alien areas of Lancashire and Durham.

Richard Brandesburton, formerly one half of the Moortown Sound machine, now divides his time between running the Keighley & Harry Worth Light Railway and running down community hospitals all across the county.

Incredibly, the Bramley Moortown studios managed to capture all of the Top Ten slots in the East Yorkshire Musical Express chart in May 1971.

The Bramley Moortown greats included Diana Rash, Stevie Blunder and Smokey Baconcrisps, who between them produced such classics as *Where Did Our Gloves Go?*, *Ain't No Slag Heap High Enough* and *I Heard It Through My Hearing Aid*.

As the label diversified it gained a fierce reputation for hiring and promoting local talent, with bands such as The Sultans of Thwing, The Rowley Stones, Gilberdyke and Sullivan, The Beverley Brothers and The Four Thorpes[4] joining soloists Anthony Newbald, Welton John and Kirk Ella Fitzgerald as part of the Moortown stable.

At one point, the label even managed to grab every one of the Top Ten slots in the *East Yorkshire Musical Express* Pop 30 Chart - quite some feat for a Leeds-based studio.

Despite the prodigious output of the Moortown Mill studios, few of the records generated much revenue for the company. It nevertheless struggled on through the late 60s, and only ceased production following a series of infamous and lengthy court battles in the 1970s, when it successfully sued both a London-based record label and a Californian manufacturer of personal computers for infringement of copyright. The resulting settlements made Hall-Road and Brandesburton so fantastically rich that they vowed never to produce another record again.

Footnotes

1. Brass bands are, alas, not appreciated by everyone. The conductor Sir Thomas Beecham once suggested that they were "are all very well in their place - outdoors and several miles away".

2. Otley, along with Ilkley, is one of the chief settlements in Wharfedale. The town boasts a particularly fine example of a butter cross, still used for its original purpose as a market site. The butter cross is seen at its best in the winter months, as in summer it is kept in the fridge. The town was frequently visited by the preacher Wesley Street, who buried his horse in the churchyard (after it died suddenly). Street would presumably have failed to get along with Thomas Chippendale, the first male stripper, who was born in the town. The Otley Chevin was an early and unsuccessful model of motor car, of which little is known.

3. From original research by T. Brooke-Taylor, J. Cleese, G. Chapman and M. Feldman.

4. The Four Thorpes are believed to have taken their name from the four villages of Thorpe, Thorpe le Street, Thorpe Hesley and Thorpe Salvin. Their recordings of *Standing in the Shadows of Loftus* and *If I Were A Blast Furnace Slagger* were popular in the area for many years.

'INABILITY' SHARP

Say the name Lancelot Sharp to anyone in Yorkshire and you might well be met with a shrug of the shoulders. Perhaps one of the lesser known members of the Sharp dynasty, Lancelot - or 'Inability' as he was invariably called at the time - nevertheless left his mark on the county, despite being one of the 18th century's least successful landscape gardeners.

Born in the village of Gawthorpe[1] to the north of Ossett in 1716, Sharp was initially apprenticed to his father[2] in the family garden centre, but swiftly moved through the ranks from junior decking monitor, through driving the miniature train, to superintendent of the pet department with special responsibility for goldfish.[3] He was also put in charge of setting up the Christmas displays every August.

Lancelot's artistic streak first manifested itself with an interest in flower arranging. He quickly created vase after vase full of artfully arranged cut flowers, many of them the right way up. Unfortunately, the flower-cutting resulted in a rather sudden and depressing fall in the garden centre's profits, and his father was forced to invite him to find employment elsewhere.

The young Lancelot was nothing if not ambitious[4] and in a short time he had secured a job working as a gardener to the aristocracy, eventually being appointed Master Gardener to King George III at Hampton Court Palace.[5] This Royal patronage brought with it fame and reputation, and Sharp was soon receiving assignments to work all over Yorkshire for noble but hard-up families who couldn't quite afford anyone else.

He favoured a style that was very different from the intricate formal gardens that had previously been the vogue. These required a great deal of work to create and maintain, whereas Lancelot's entirely natural-looking landscapes frequently needed only minimal work on his part and, wherever possible, none at all.

His first major commission was at Heckmondwike Hall, traditional seat of the Dukes of Gomersal. Here, the elderly 8th duke complained that the view from his study was uniformly dull, grey and uninspiring. Lancelot identified the problem immediately and, having arranged for the windows to be cleaned, gained both the old duke's favour and rather a lot of his cash.

Other projects he completed proved to be more demanding. His remodelling of Todmorden Towers,[6] for example, involved the relocation of an entire

Inability Sharp's liking for follies often led to an over-exuberant reliance on them in his formal garden designs.

community which was offending the discerning eye of the Marquis of Mytholmroyd. In what was regarded by some as an over-reaction, Lancelot organised the removal of the entire village of Fauquembergues from West Yorkshire to northern France, where it remains to this day.

It was at Todmorden Towers that Sharp first made use of the 'a Ha', an idea that he stole from a Norwegian he met in Horten Market.[7] It made perfect sense to Sharp to combine a fjord with a ski-jump, despite never having seen either. Falling down the resulting, huge, invisible ditch which completely encircled the house instantly killed any humans or livestock who ventured nearby and imprisoned the Marquis in his home for the next 19 years. In desperation (the wine cellar having finally run dry), he was eventually able to tunnel his way to freedom.[8]

Lancelot was very fond of creating features that could catch the eye in his landscapes, and would often build elaborate follies, his favourites being mock ruins placed in appropriate places on the edges of his parks. It was this fondness that would bring a regrettable end to his career.

Sharp's plans for the remodelling of Castleford House, home to the Earl of Normanton, were magnificent. The great house would stand at the northern end of the new park. From it, the Earl and his guests would see a magnificent sweep of rolling grassland, carefully placed clumps of trees, a winding ornamental lake and, silhouetted against the southern horizon, a romantic, weather beaten ivy-clad ruin.

By this time in his career, Lancelot was busier with work than ever, and it appears that his notes for the contractors were added to the site plan somewhat hastily. More specifically, the sketch was, it appears, upside-down when he appended the words 'Create ruin here' to it.

It is said that the Earl arrived home from a grand tour of Europe just in time to see the last cartload of spare stones trundling away from what had until recently been his ancestral home, and which was now a good deal more romantic, if a great deal less habitable.

Lancelot Sharp's reputation never fully recovered, and he retired to Ossett, to his garden, where he ended his days cultivating roses and, less successfully, goldfish.

Footnotes

1. Although technically now part of Ossett, Gawthorpe is noted as one of only two villages in Yorkshire to possess a maypole.[i] It also, in the face of stiff competition from Sydney and Rio de Janeiro, hosts the world coal-carrying championships.

2. A man of diminutive stature, known to his friends as Alan 'Titch' Sharp.

3. In this role he came in for criticism from animal rights activists for making it insufficiently clear to his staff that the creatures were not to be planted.

4. He was certainly ambitious. Unfortunately, he wasn't anything much else.

5. Named, by the eccentric monarch, in commemoration of an unfortunate and painful incident with a zip fastener.

6. Controversy - or perhaps some degree of mild confusion - surrounds the name of the village of Todmorden. One theory claims that the name means 'Totta's boundary valley', another that the derivation is 'Marshy home of the fox'. One particularly cheerful source has suggested that it means 'Death-Death Wood', although one of the first acts of the town's tourist authorities was to tear down the signs bearing this name. Up to late Victorian times Todmorden straddled the Yorkshire/Lancashire border, although since 1888 it has been officially located[ii] in Yorkshire. The fact that many inhabitants consider themselves Lancastrian, that it has an Oldham postcode, and its sporting teams play in Lancashire leagues are of minor consequence.

7. Other, less ambitious, gardeners contented themselves with a much smaller wall-and-ditch arrangement, which was sneered at by Sharp, who referred to it derisively as a 'ha-ha'.

8. An event later immortalised in J. Arthur Rival's 1955 epic *The Cold Ditch Story*, starring John Stuart Mill.

Sub-Footnotes

i. The other is Barwick in Elmet.[a] In 1924, Yorkshire composer Arnold Wood celebrated the village in a piece of maypole[b] dance music called *Candlewick Green*. This is better known today as the theme tune to the popular West Yorks TV children's programme *Candlewick Green*.

ii. 'Annexed by' is the term preferred in Lancashire.

Sub-Sub-Footnotes

a. Elmet was an ancient Celtic kingdom, named after the protective headgear the ancient Celtic people wore to go with their green and white hooped shirts.

b. The purpose of maypoles remains unclear. Some believe they are relics of early tree worship, but are unable to explain how the early tree worshippers stopped their ribbons getting tangled in the branches. Others, including Ossett psychotherapist Sigmund Sharp, believe there are phallic connotations.

HULL

One of Britain's most proudly individual cities (or perhaps one of Britain's most vaguely eccentric, depending on whether or not you live there) lies at the end of the Silk Road[1] in the mysterious far east of Yorkshire.

Nestling on the mighty river Humber and having been named 'Kings town' by Edward I, it felt natural to its contrary inhabitants to ignore both names and refer to their city as Hull, after the small and muddy river[2] that flows through its centre [3] (when it has been naughty, of course, it is given its full name of Kingston upon Hull, spoken in a very stern voice).

Hull's growth as a port burgeoned with the export of flat caps, whippets and unripened rhubarb.[4] The wool for the caps came from the nearby estates of Meaux Abbey, which was bordered on three sides by Beverley and its twin sister towns, Teddie and Babs. Meaux Abbey monks dyed the wool with locally-grown Burberries and fashioned it into Yorkshire's most famous headgear.

There were at least 120 roads into Hull at this time, all of them based on well-established Drovers' roads, where packs of whippets were 'droved' from market towns to Hull. This trade made the abbey and the town very rich indeed, a circumstance which did not go unnoticed by King

At its peak, the Hanseatic League (of which Hull was briefly a member) covered most of the coast of north west Europe and contained over 30 different teams.

Edward I who bought[5] the town from the monks (who were unaware that it was up for sale). In 1299, he granted it a royal charter that, just to make the point crystal clear, renamed the place "King's Town, you hear what I'm saying guys, upon Hull", although the central portion of this name was generally abandoned after Edward's death.

Hull continued to prosper, initially exporting goods from Yorkshire, but gradually expanding to export goods from every county of England, Scotland and Wales (except Lancashire, where a 500% border tariff made transportation costs prohibitive). Hull's docking expertise was also used on the ships' return trips and

Hull's distinctive cream telephone boxes: technical difficulties in the early days required these to be placed no more than 10 yards apart.

Hull became a key centre for the import of wine, timber and fake perfume.

For most of the middle ages, Hull was a busy member of the Hanseatic League, finishing third in the 1471-72 season, but being relegated the following year. Hull supported Cromwell during the early part of the English Civil War, and as a result was besieged by Royalist forces, since both sides were anxious to have access to Hull's large arsenal. The arsenal was also a member of the Hanseatic League, and finished fourth on goal difference every year for almost two centuries.

However, not all Hull's prosperity resulted from such relatively reputable business. In the 19th century, Hull had a large and enthusiastically active whaling fleet. There was also some involvement with the slave trade, although Hull was not as guilty as Bristol or Liverpool in this respect, partly because it faced east towards Europe, rather than west towards the Americas, and partly because it quickly transpired that whales were singularly inept at picking cotton. Both activities only came to an end with the appointment of Charles & Maurice Spaatchcock as the city council's public relations advisors.

Hull residents are rightly proud of their privately-owned telephone system, which they keep separate from the rest of the country's. Hull residents are also proud of the part that alum played in this development: when access to Italian alum (essential as a fixative for dying textiles) was cut off following the Reformation, shale from the Yorkshire coast was found to be an acceptable substitute. However, the production process required a steady supply of urine, so to meet this need public toilets were built in Hull to serve as the collection points.

Alum production has, of course, gone the way of much manufacturing industry, removing the need for this collection. Rather than dismantle the conveniences, far-sighted city fathers had them converted to the profusion of cream-coloured telephone boxes now scattered about the city. Proud of their heritage, many Hull residents continue to commemorate their original purpose, especially on a Saturday night whilst waiting for a taxi.

During the Second World War, Hull discovered to its dismay that being a major industrial city and port, on a large and unmistakeable estuary facing Germany was not an unobtrusive position Luftwaffe-wise. The city centre was largely rebuilt after the war, but unexploded munitions continued to turn up in inconvenient circumstances for many years afterwards.[6]

The outskirts of Hull today include a number of formerly isolated villages, one of which, Cottingham[7] claims to be both Britain's largest, small village and Britain's smallest, large village.

In 1981, those of Hessle's 15,000 villagers who wanted to visit friends or relatives in the even smaller Barton-on-Humber were finally able to do so by the construction of the £98 million Humber Bridge,[8] which even many locals considered an unusually expensive effort to improve their transport links.

In 2017 Hull followed Derry-Londonderry as the second UK City of Culture. Whether it will therefore have to be referred to as Hull-Kingstonuponhull is undecided at the time of going to press.

Footnotes

1. Actually more of a 97% Wool / 3% Viscose Road.

2. The course of the River Hull is almost all at, or only slightly above, sea level, and the lands surrounding it have been prone to flooding for centuries. "Good" thought the founders surveying the remote and soggy fields. "Ideal spot to build a city...".

3. Not content with shortening the name to Hull, the economical locals tend to refer to 'Ol'.

4. Ripe rhubarb quickly turned to pulp in the holds of boats, until a method was discovered of spraying the green stems with red dye to make them look ripe.[i]

5. By means of a sort of 13th century Compulsory Purchase Order, backed up by a lot of men with swords.

6. As recently as 2006, an archive document was found suggesting that, unbeknownst to the developers, a large unexploded bomb was probably buried under the proposed site of a major new leisure and housing complex in Hull. At the time, the development (later abandoned) was to have been called 'The Boom'. It was described in promotional literature as 'an explosive experience in urban living'.

7. Cottingham hosts an annual 'Springboard Festival' to showcase up and coming local musical talent. Due to a misunderstanding in 2012, the absence of water meant that a number of aspiring Olympic high divers sadly came to painful grief.

8. At the time of its completion in 1981 the Humber Bridge was the longest single-span suspension bridge in the world. As of 2017, however, it was only the seventh longest. This is generally attributed to plate tectonics, which are gradually moving Lincolnshire closer to the East Riding

Sub-Footnote

i. The red dye, although poisonous, produced a mild tingling taste, which most people professed to prefer to rhubarb, prior to expiring.

THE WETWANG
POND MONSTER

Today, the picturesque Wolds village of Wetwang[1] is a quiet stop on the busy A166 road to Bridlington, and chiefly famous for the black swans on the Bottom Pond.[2] These birds can be observed from the vicinity of *The Black Swan* public house, and the uncanny coincidence of the name has often been noted by the superstitiously inclined.

But it is a now mainly forgotten that, for many years, rumours circulated amongst local folk of a far more mysterious creature associated with the village pond. Lurking in the unfathomed depths, 'Wettie', as the beast came to be called, was also believed by some to inhabit these same waters.

The earliest report of a monster associated with the pond came in the words of Yorkshire's famed historian and knucklehead Arthur of Rievaulx. In one of his infrequent breaks from brewing (and enthusiastically sampling) Byland Tonic Wine[3] Arthur writes that the Irish saint Christopher O'Columbus[4] (the patron saint of travellers' cheques) was returning one evening from a pilgrimage to the fish and chip shops of Whitby when he happened to pass through Wetwang. Seeing a commotion by the pond, he stopped to ask the cause, and was told that a local duck had been seriously

The pond at Wetwang.

molested by a "water beast" that had almost dragged her under.

O'Columbus acted swiftly. Turning to a companion[5] (to whom he owed money) he ordered the man into the water. Immediately there was a loud splashing, and a terrible creature was seen approaching through the dusk. But O'Columbus raised his arms, made the sign of the cross, and ordered the beast to retreat. Some say he also sprinkled a little holy water, but all agree that whatever he did, it worked, and the creature turned and fled.[6] And there matters might have rested; but tales handed down in the pub, along with occasional late-night sightings by those leaving it, ensured that the legend was to live on for many generations.

Interest in the monster increased once more in the early twentieth century, when better transport, private cars and a series of guide books published by the East Riding Tourist Development Committee brought more and more tourists to (or at any rate, through) Wetwang. By then, some would have had cameras, and so eventually the first photographic 'evidence' of Wettie was captured.

The photograph was grainy and out-of-focus, and gave every indication of having been taken from a distance, in a hurry, by an agitated man balancing on a trampoline in thick fog. Nonetheless, it did appear to show a strange and unidentifiable creature with a long, black, swan-like neck protruding from the water, and many people, including members of the Wetwang low-visibility amateur gymnastics club, were convinced that it could only be a photograph of the fabled monster.

Taken by a local Baronet, 'Sir John's Photograph' (as it became known) was widely publicised, and curious visitors flocked to the village, eventually necessitating the construction of Yorkshire's only multi-storey charabanc park. On summer days, the banks of the pond would be thronged with eager visitors, each hoping to catch a glimpse of the fabled creature. The fact that no-one ever did failed to dampen their enthusiasm, and indeed tourists were further encouraged by the host of additional attractions that the good, not to say avaricious, folk of Wetwang laid on for their visitors.[7]

By the 1960s though, alternative forms of entertainment were taking their toll on Wettie's popularity. The ready availability of various illegal substances meant that sights far more remarkable than a mere aquatic monster could be 'seen', although North Yorkshire's popular musical combo The Bedales did pay eloquent tribute to the

'Sir John's Photograph' of a creature with a long, black, swan-like neck was the cause of crowds of the curious flocking to Wetwang.

monster in their 1967 single *Wettie in the Pond with Diazepam*.

One of the last to take a serious interest was the famous naturalist and inventor of the woggle, Sir Peter Scout. Deploying the latest scientific techniques, Scout's team scoured the pond (a number of locals said afterwards that they had never seen it quite so clean) and eventually announced to the world that they had evidence of the creature's existence, in the form of a blurred photograph of a flipper. As ever with Wettie, this proved controversial, and members of the Wetwang and Garton-on-the-Wolds snorkelling club, who had been holding their annual meet at the time, insisted they had seen nothing unusual.

And so, today, all is calm in the village. Ask the average passer-by whether they have ever had a Wettie encounter, and they tend to respond with a strange (not to say worried) look. But late at night, behind the bus shelter, some say that odd sounds and terrible sights can still be heard and seen.

The legend lives on...

Footnotes

1. Debate continues to surround the origin of the name 'Wetwang'[i]. Some say that the name simply means 'Wet Field', and point to Driffield, just up the road, as a contrast. More ambitiously, others say it derives from the Viking 'Vertvanger, meaning 'field for the trial of a legal action', although why one field might be significantly more useful than another for such purposes remains unclear.

2. The Bottom Pond is so-named in order to distinguish it from the Top Pond, which doesn't exist.

3. Byland Tonic Wine, also known as 'Bye-bye', 'Yorkshire Marching Juice', and 'Monks Revenge' was a powerful potion brewed from a mix of crab apples, methylated spirits and old tyres.[ii] Over the years some of the more imaginative historians have blamed it for a number of spontaneous outbreaks of violence including the sacking of Rome, the Wars of the Roses, and regular brawls in Keighley.

4. Saint O'Columbus is noted as the founder of the great monastery on the remote Scottish island of Ikea, famous for the production flat-packed pews and self-assembly altars which were exported to the farthest corners of the Christian world.

5. Widely believed to have been St.Elios, founder and managing director of EasyPilgrim.[iii]

6. A more recent theory is that what he sprinkled was actually Byland Tonic Wine, and the poor monster simply wasn't up to it.

7. These included Wettie-land (a number of papier-mâché models of the creature, displayed in a tin bath inside an old barn) and the famous Wettie-cruises, which consisted of a trip the length of the pond in a huge, swan-shaped pedalo liberated one night from a Bridlington amusement park.

Sub-Footnotes

i. For several years, Channel 4's *Countdown* host Richard 'Twice Nightly' Whiteley was honorary Mayor of Wetwang.

ii. *Last of the Tonic Wine*, a sitcom featuring three elderly tramps living in a park in Keighley, ran for three seasons on the cable channel West Riding Community TV, until poor viewing figures caused the station to drop the series.

iii. No frills pilgrimages and crusades; Holy water an additional extra.

SCARBOROUGH

Scarborough is Yorkshire's largest seaside resort, and is even said by some more imaginative observers to be the world's first.[1]

'Skarðaborg' is reputed to have been founded in 966 by a Viking, Thorgils Skarthi, who had evidently grown tired of demolishing other people's towns, and decided to have a go at building one of his own. This seems to have outraged his colleagues, and one Tostig Godwinson reverted to traditional practice and burnt it down again.[2] Thus, at the time in 1085 when William the Conqueror's surveyors reached 'S' in the Domesday Book[3] there was, as the great document records, 'naffe all' to be listed, as much of the town lay in ruins.

Two English monarchs were responsible for Scarborough's later recovery. King Henry II built a small castle on the beach, but unfortunately the tide came in, so instead he built a much larger one on the headland that dominates the town. Edward II subsequently granted Scarborough Castle to his particular friend Piers Gaveston,[4] who eventually became so influential that a number of murderous barons intervened, after which much of Gaveston lay in ruins.[5]

In the 13th century, a Royal Charter granted Scarborough the right to hold a great trading fair (or 'Fayre', as the antique dealers and olde tea shoppes preferred it) which lasted for 500 years, by which time the beer tent really had run out. This event is of course commemorated in the song *Scarborough Fair:*[6] Scarborough then changed hands several times during the English Civil War, following which much of the town lay (once again) in ruins.

In the 17th century. a local lady found water flowing from beneath the cliff to the south of the town. Noting that this water was staining the rock an unsightly red-brown colour, she unaccountably failed to call the environmental heath inspectors and instead tasted the water. Acting on the 'cough-mixture principal' (anything that tastes so bad must be good for you)[7] she announced its virtues to the world, and those suffering from a bad case of nothing better to do were soon flocking to the town. By the early 1700s business was so good that a predecessor of the present day Spa complex had been constructed, but after a major cliff-fall in 1737, much of the site lay in ruins.[8]

By 1858, the Spa had become a considerable development, with new buildings designed by Joseph 'The Inflammable' Paxton,[9] the architect of the Crystal Palace, whilst in 1875 a funicular railway[10] was built to connect it with the esplanade on the cliff top. Unaccountably, the following year witnessed a bad fire after which much of the site (though sadly not the career of Paxton) lay in ruins.

Earlier, in 1845, Scarborough had acquired both its first hotel, and a railway link to York,[11] and visitor numbers grew throughout the Victorian era. During the First World War, the town and the castle were bombarded by German warships (as was nearby Whitby Abbey) after which much of the site lay in ruins.

A particular characteristic of the town has always been the way in which the promontory on which the castle stands, effectively divides the seafront into two, the North and South bays. This was an especially attractive feature to Yorkshire holidaymakers, the prospect of two bays for the price of one proving almost irresistible.

The South Bay is dominated by the Grand Hotel which, when completed in 1867, was one of the largest hotels in the world. Its four towers represented the seasons, 12 floors the months, 52 chimneys the weeks and 365 bedrooms the days of the year. However, the early custom of building and demolishing a leap-bedroom every fourth year is no longer practised.[12]

The North Bay is noted in particular for the Japanese-themed Peasholm Park,[13] complete with its own pagoda and oriental bridge.[14] The park's lake is regularly used to present a model re-enactment of the Battle of the River Plate, and of all the world's imitation South American naval encounters in Japanese surroundings, this is frequently said to be the most realistic.

Scarborough, a town which has always had a special— if somewhat unfathomable—attraction for Yorkshire folk.

Scarborough gained worldwide attention most recently in 1993, when a landslip caused part of the Holbeck Hall Hotel to fall into the sea. After which the remainder of the hotel lay in ruins.

Footnotes

1. This claim is hotly disputed, for example by Blackpool and Brighton. But what would you expect from Lancastrians and Southerners?

2. The suggestion that the town was then revived again by Sandi Toksvig, a small beach-loving Viking, has no apparent foundation.

3. The name of the book is not, as commonly supposed, related to 'Doomsday'. In fact, it comes from the Latin *Domestos*, meaning to tax 99% of all known peasants.

4. Historians believe that it was around this time that the phrase 'Queen of the East Coast' was first used in a Scarborough-related context.

5. Piers Gaveston appears to have visited a large number of seaside towns in his career, since many still have large

horizontal erections named in his honour He also gave his name to a popular brand of indigestion tablet.

6. Note to budding songwriters: if you're struggling with a line, just bung 'Parsley, Sage, Rosemary and Thyme' in there at random. It works every time:

'When I find myself in times of trouble
Parsley, Sage, Rosemary and Thyme'

'Is this the real life,
Is this just fantasy,
Caught in a landslide,
Parsley, Sage, Rosemary and Thyme'

'How many roads must a man walk down
Parsley, Sage, Rosemary and Thyme'

7. 'Tastes Like it's Good For You!' was the strapline for a magazine ad promoted by the British Tripe Council in 1957.

8. That it reopened in only a few weeks points to the extraordinary popularity of drinking diluted battery acid in this period.

9. Paxton's Crystal Palace was, of course, a huge building made almost entirely from glass and iron, whilst Scarborough Spa was specifically designed to house lots of water. Both somehow managed to burn down.

10. The exact shade is unknown, but in fact most visitors appear to have considered it a perfectly normal colour.

11. Scarborough station boasts the longest railway station bench in the world. At 139 metres it is capable of seating over 60 American tourists in comfort.

12. Betjeman Sharp (see pp. 23-25) was famously barred from the hotel after writing that '24 hours represents the longest anyone should ever stay in this unlovely place and 60 minutes the waiting time between ordering a meal and its arrival.'

13. Peasholm Park forms part of the estate of the Manor of Northstead. Stewardship of the manor, like that of the better known Chiltern Hundreds, is a post that MPs apply for when they wish to resign and do something useful. It carries no salary and has no duties, but is a useful way of keeping the unemployment figures down.

14. The number of Yorkshire-themed gardens in Japan is not currently known.

THE LEGEND OF COUNT DRACIBIRD

Supernatural figures, ghosts, ogres, boggarts and the like, have always been part of Yorkshire legend, and even, perhaps, of Yorkshire fact. But no legend has bitten more deeply into the county's folk memory than the eerie story of Count Dracibird - the notorious Umpire.[1]

Our story begins on a cold and foggy night in Whitby. The pungent and greasy steam from dozens of fish and chip shops[2] rose into the still air and wrapped itself around the ruins of the famous abbey,[3] perched high on its headland. Gas lamps could barely pierce the Dickensian[4] gloom, and the scent of hot vinegar hung heavy over the town.

A number of old salts were gathered in one of the pubs, drinking off the effects of a heavy night's fish and chip crawl. The chief topic of discussion was the arrival in the harbour that day of a mysterious ship, that some said had come all the way from Australia.

Suddenly, a terrible howl was heard. Looking out of the door, they beheld a great black dog, eyes as large as pickled eggs, padding along the quay. The men watched in horror as, pausing only to cock its leg against a lamp post, the unearthly creature bounded up the famous 199 steps[5] to the abbey, and disappeared into the mist.

Whitby Abbey, glimpsed through the swirl of fish and chip fumes.

It was shortly afterwards that rumours of a strange apparition began to be heard. Whitby's Ladies of the Night[6] began to report sightings of a short figure in a flat cap and a long white coat appearing in the lamplight. It was said to slowly raise its right forefinger before fading into the mist.

After a while, though, these sightings became less frequent, and Whitby was at peace once again. And there the story of Count Dracibird might have ended, except that his most terrifying manifestation was yet to come...

Our story now moves south, to the mining town of Barnsley.[7] Owing to their regular umpire's guide dog having contracted rickets, the cricket club found itself short of a match official, and a kindly, if rather long in the tooth, stranger offered his services.[8] Ignoring the fact that the newcomer appeared to have mis-understood the purpose of bats in a cricketing context, and had a pipistrelle struggling to escape from his coat pocket, the two captains accepted the offer, and the match began.

For the first few overs, the game followed the normal course of a Yorkshire cricket match, the opening batsmen carefully defending their wickets and doing their utmost not to provoke unseemly excitement in the sparse crowd by scoring runs.[9]

Before long though, events took an unheard-of turn. In the 13th over, an unusually accurate ball struck the batsman, one E.C. Egan, on the pad. At the same time the bowler, noticing the unfamiliar new umpire for the first time, enquired of a fielder, "Who's that?"

Did the umpire mishear? Or was it simply sufficient pretext? Whatever the case, it was enough. To the astonishment of all, the stranger raised his finger, and Egan was out!

An awed hush fell over the crowd, the silence broken only by the soft thud of old ladies hitting the turf as they fainted.

Never in the history of Yorkshire cricket had a man been given out on the first day. And certainly not lbw![10]

But the strange umpire only smiled inscrutably. There was now a problem. It being so early in the match, the number three batsman had not yet considered it necessary to put on his pads. Or don his cricket whites. Or indeed turn up, and in point of fact was still only half-way through a 19 hour shift on the thin seam of Grimethorpe colliery.[11]

The mutterings in the crowd were growing louder, when the day was saved by the local vicar. Quickly strapping on spare pads, he strode purposefully to the wicket and, as if in tribute to the man of God, for the first time that season, the sun broke briefly through the clouds.

Taking his guard, he turned to the umpire, and as he did so sunlight glinted gently on the crucifix around his neck.

The effect was immediate. With a terrible howl, Dracibird bared his three monstrous fangs, and leaped down the wicket at the unfortunate clergyman. But the vicar was equal to him, and snatching a stump from the ground he hurled it at his attacker, piercing him through the heart.

As the onlookers watched in horror, Dracibird fell to his knees, and with a last despairing cry of "Out!" the umpire crumbled away into dust and ashes[12] and a terrible pall of smoke rose to the heavens.

In view of this, the match was abandoned due to bad light.[13]

.

Footnotes

1. Much of the material for this account has been shamelessly plagiarised from *Myths, Legends and Downright Lies of Yorkshire*, by Stan Broker (Fable and Fable, 1951). Although long out of print, copies of this sought-after publication can occasionally be discovered in rare book auctions, charity shops or skips.

2. The centre of Whitby today consists almost entirely of fish and chip shops, separated only by the occasional pub. It was to satisfy the demand created by these establishments that a major fishing industry grew up in the town. Its pioneer was the famous explorer-turned-chef, Captain Cook. Whitby also had a substantial whaling fleet, and whales too were served in chippys throughout Yorkshire, where they were known as 'Specials'.

3. Whitby Abbey was founded in 657AD by St. Hilda of Hartlepool.[i]   In 664,[ii] the Synod of Whitby fixed the date of Easter as the first Sunday after the first full moon on or after the March equinox, thus ensuring that no-one ever knew quite when to book their annual leave. A few years later the Sinex of Whitby invented the nasal decongestant.

4. Charles Dickens was in fact a frequent visitor to Whitby, and on one occasion addressed the local Women's Institute. However, the rumour that one of the ladies, on being asked "Do you like Dickens?" replied "I don't know, I've never been to one" is probably false.

5. There are some who maintain that in fact there are only 198 steps, as the final one, being at the top, doesn't count as a step. These people are tiresome pedants who should on no account be encouraged. A local bye-law (only repealed in 2003) previously allowed them to be hurled bodily back down the steps again.

6. These women made a precarious living by supplying 'extra services' to late-night fish and chip consumers. They were known as 'Tarts', short for 'Tartares', after the most popular product amongst southern tourists.

7. In addition to its part in the story of Count Dracibird, Barnsley has many other claims to fame. The municipal gardener-turned-chat-show-host Michael Parkinsharp (so tragically maimed live on-air after making unwanted advances to an emu) hails from the town, whilst the nearby village of Havercroft gives its name to the form of air-cushioned land-or-sea transport developed there by Sir Christopher Cockandbull.

8. This, in itself, ought to have aroused suspicion. Since the likelihood of a Yorkshireman offering his services free of charge is remote, the stranger must surely have been an 'off-comed 'un'.

9. No-one epitomised the spirit of Yorkshire cricket at the time better than Jeremy Boyclott. Noted for his ability to occupy the crease for days on end without actually moving, in the course of a more than 20 year career he ~~averaged~~ scored almost 100 runs.

10. It being a subjective decision, no Yorkshire umpire would ever wish to disturb the solemnity of a match by giving a man out leg before wicket. Even the most blatant forms of dismissal, such as all three stumps having been sent cart wheeling down the ground, could usually be dealt with by a strategic call of "no ball".

11. Immortalised in the J. Arthur Rival classic tale of an aristocrat who sets up his own band, *Brass Toff*.

12. The ashes are said to have been collected and placed in a little urn, which predated Morecambe and Wise by many decades. And from that day to this, it has been the trophy traditionally won by Australia whenever they play England at cricket.

13. The events related here were dramatised in J. Arthur Rival's 1973 production *The Wicket Man*.

Sub-Footnotes

i. Betty of Billingham was allegedly off sick that day.

ii. The number 664 is traditionally referred to as 'The Neighbour of the Beast'.

CHESTERFIELD

Although this book concerns itself mainly with Yorkshire, I am told that there are interesting places just outside the county's boundaries which it would be a shame to ignore.[1] One such place is Chesterfield.

Technically the town is in Derbyshire, although the friendly natives tend to loudly insist that they are in <u>North</u> Derbyshire, and have nothing to do with Derby. They will then further add that there's nothing much wrong with Derby, it's just that Chesterfield is better and more friendly.

Unfortunately, the friendliness tends not to extend back over the Yorkshire border to Sheffield, whose inhabitants are generally referred to (at best) as 'dee-dahs'.[2] However, this is still mild when compared to some of the abuse heaped upon Mansfield and its citizens. But apart from these little local rivalries, it's a friendly town, they insist.

Chesterfield was granted its market charter by King John in 1204. This is unusual as John was not generally fond of charters, and it usually needed a deal of persuading by a lot of barons to make him set his name to one.[3] Nonetheless, the market continues in the town to this day, and the market square is reckoned to be one of the squarest in the country. Many of the second-hand stalls may well still

A spire.

of the second-hand stalls may well still carry original stock, though not, alas, at original prices.

Chesterfield's most notable feature dates from a little later than this. The spire of St. Mary and All Saints church is famously twisted. Various technical explanations have been given for this, but folklore has it that a blacksmith in Bolsover[4] failed to fit the Devil's shoes properly and, whilst hopping around in pain, he (the Devil) knocked the spire out of shape. What he subsequently did to the blacksmith is, perhaps fortunately, not recorded.[5]

The town has, nevertheless, adopted this peculiarity as a badge of honour, and for many years it has been illegal under a local bylaw to open a business in Chesterfield that does not have the word 'Spire' in its name – and the town motto on its coat of arms is 'Aspire'.

Several shops and market stalls in Chesterfield compete to sell Derbyshire Oatcakes. These small, flat pancakes are made from oatmeal, flour and yeast, and (you will be told, with friendly impatience) are completely different from, and much superior to, Staffordshire Oatcakes, which by contrast are made from oatmeal, flour and yeast.[6]

Chesterfield's disdain is not reserved solely for other towns or foodstuffs. To this day, mention of the former football referee Mr. David Elleray is accompanied by the sort of facial expression normally found on someone who has bitten into a sour lemon thinking it was a ripe peach.[7]

Communication in Chesterfield can occasionally be problematic for English speakers. Attempt to purchase a sandwich, and you might well be asked 'Would you like a cob, duck?', at which point outsiders of a nervous disposition, unused to being spontaneously offered an unknown species of aquatic fowl have been known to go outside for a little sit down.

What these poor souls know not, is that what the outside world might refer to as a bread roll, bread cake, or even teacake is, in Chesterfield, a cob. And in Derbyshire (including North Derbyshire!), 'duck' is a generic friendly term, on a par with 'love' in Yorkshire.

And herein lies the mystery. You will never be called 'duck' in Sheffield, you will never be called anything else in Chesterfield. So what, and where, is the boundary? Is there a white line painted on the ground between Coal Aston and Killamarsh? A dyke near Dronfield? A Woodseats wall? Are strict punishments imposed by the friendly folk of Chesterfield on miscreants who inadvertently say 'love'?

My research is still ongoing. But in the meantime, one piece of advice can safely be offered to Yorkshire folk and their visitors. If they call you 'duck' you've strayed beyond the spiritual boundaries of Yorkshire. Things are different. Just look at that church.

Footnotes

1. Not the least because my publisher has insisted that I widen the scope of this book beyond the borders of Yorkshire, in an attempt (I can only surmise) to increase its sales.

2. On account of their accent – "Dey don't say thee 'n' tha, dey say dee and dah the stupid dee-dahs". Allegedly.

3. The most successful strategy was to get him drunk on runny mead.

4. Bolsover is a nearby village which seems also to have incurred Chesterfield's displeasure in the past. The locals call it 'Bozer'. Chesterfield's claim that this is 'because they can't manage three syllables' is almost certainly slanderous.

5. Natives have a further explanation for the twist in the spire. They say that not long after the church was built in the 14th century, a virgin was married in it, and the spire was so surprised that it leaned over for a closer look. Furthermore, the next time a virgin is married there, it will straighten up again. However, as it's only been around for 700 years, this hasn't happened yet.

6. Not far from Chesterfield is the small town of Bakewell, which is definitely *not*, as you might carelessly assume, the home of the Bakewell Tart. The product, you will be firmly advised, is a Bakewell *Pudding* and, to prove it, the town is home to the one-and-only original Bakewell Pudding Shop. There are two of them.[i]

7. In 1997, a highly dubious[ii] decision by Mr. Elleray probably denied Chesterfield FC[iii] a place in the FA Cup Final. They would have been the first club from the third tier of the leagues to get there.

Sub-Footnotes

i. It goes without saying that the almost inedible black discs produced as a by product of fracking for parkin near the little hamlet of Ponty should really be known as Ponty frack lozenges, not cakes.

ii. i.e. dead wrong.

iii. Chesterfield FC are nicknamed The Spireites. Inevitably.

THE KEITH LEIGH & HARRY WORTH RAILWAY

Part of Yorkshire's rich and undoubtedly colourful transport history lives and thrives today, in the form of the famous Keith Leigh and Harry Worth[1] Railway.

Keith Leigh and Harry Worth were early enthusiasts for the work of the famous Bluntë sisters of Haworth. As discussed in an earlier publication, (*Forgotten Lancashire and Parts of Cheshire and the Wirral*), the Bluntë's were brought up in the parsonage at Haworth where, surrounded by soot-blackened tombstones and with views of the desolate, windswept bleakness of the moors, they developed the naturally cheery and light hearted outlook which was to characterise much of their work.

When Leigh and Worth attempted to visit Haworth in 1861, they were surprised to find that the village had no train service, and were unsatisfied with the explanation that this was because there was no railway.[2] Being Victorians, they immediately resolved to build a railway themselves, but then had second thoughts and decided that perhaps they'd just pay a lot of other people not very much money to build it for them.[3]

Construction of the line was plagued with difficulties. When a cow ate the plans of the line it occurred to everyone all at the same time that it might have been a good idea to have a second set. The building of Ingrow Tunnel was hampered by the fact that everyone thought it was a painful foot condition, and the work also caused the local Methodist chapel to subside into the river, prompting a quick change of denomination to Baptist.

For a century the line served the valley, bringing coal from the south of Yorkshire to the mills, and taking away finished fine woollens, sometimes in different trucks. There was also a steady flow of visitors to the Haworth Parsonage Experience Theme Park and House of Fun.[4]

By the 1960s, however, the railway was in decline. More and more people owned their own cars, and were thus quick to take the opportunity to go somewhere other than Haworth. The mills were in decline, due in part to controversial social experiments such as the abolition of child labour and introduction of the 70 hour week. And so the Beecham[5] Axe fell on the line, derailing a train and prompting closure.

Happily though, this was not the end. Enough people were nostalgic for the delights of old-fashioned rail travel[6] for a preservation society to be formed by local rail enthusiasts, who also volunteered to operate the line.[7]

The railway received a huge boost when it was selected by the J. Arthur Rival Studios as the location for their 1970 family blockbuster *The Train Brats*.[8] This follows the fortunes of three uncontrollable hooligans who try to wreck a train in order to draw attention to the plight of their father who has been justly imprisoned for various unspecified offences. In the famous climactic scene, he attempts unsuccessfully to jump a barbed wire fence in a small tank engine.

Today, the railway continues to operate, providing a nostalgic breath of smoky and not particularly fresh air for thousands of visitors.

Footnotes

1. Harry Worth was the grandfather of the well known 1960s TV comedian, Henry Worth. The younger Worth was famed for the astonishing act of levitation he performed in a shop doorway, which was filmed and used as the opening sequence for his shows. Paranormal investigators including Uri Gullible and the Indian mystic Derek Pakora still consider this feat to be completely inexplicable.

2. They eventually reached the village on bicycles hired from a local cycle shop proprietor, Miss Penelope Farthing.

3. Like almost all Victorian railways, the line was constructed by navvies.[i] These men were extremely industrious, strong and fit, but were also notorious for being lawless, violent, hard-drinking, ill-disciplined and quick to take offence. As such they were looked down on by the locals who considered them somewhat effeminate. It was only after a number of skirmishes that they were left in peace to construct the railway.

4. In 1953, the Haworth Parsonage Experience Theme Park and House of Fun was voted Yorkshire's second favourite visitor attraction.[ii]

5. Dr. Robert Beecham was a successful businessman and noted industrialist. He was the founder of a number of major companies, including Beecham Beattie Road Builders Ltd, the Beecham Bus Company, and Beecham's Locomotive Scrapyard. With this excellent track record, it was only natural that the government should appoint him chairman of the British Railways Board, with the brief of producing an impartial report on the future of the railways. When *The Mis-shaping of British Railways* appeared its proposals proved controversial, as less than 30 miles of railway would have been left, coincidentally connecting Dr. Beecham's home and office.

6. These included not being able to lower the window to open the door before the train departed, getting smoke in your eyes because you then couldn't close the window again, and being imprisoned in a non-corridor compartment with a Jehovah's Witness.

7. It was felt that with only two engines to start with, the attractions of simply 'spotting' and number-collecting would start to pall after a few weeks.

8. This film is noted by connoisseurs for the controversial appearance of actress Ms Ginny Agate who, in a move believed to be unique in her career, retained her clothing throughout.

Sub-Footnotes

i. 'Navvies were so-named because of the Navvy blue jerseys they were obliged to wear whilst constructing the first short canal sections, which were known as 'navigations' because they enabled navigators of river boats to navigate past un-navigable sections of river.

ii. The Keighley Abattoir Experience was voted number one.

YORKSHIRE'S GREAT DETECTIVE

Of all Yorkshire's great but largely disregarded characters, few can have had mightier intellectual ability than Shirley Ockholmes, arguably perhaps the greatest female detective of her age.

Born in Mytholmroyd[1] in 1854, Shirley (or 'Shirl', as she was invariably called) was a daughter of the Ockholmes clan, one of the many large and lawless families that inhabited the wild Lancashire borderlands for centuries. However, by the mid 19th century things had calmed down (a bit) and the Ockholmes' had established a large and lucrative gravy-browning factory on the outskirts of Hebden Bridge, which made full use of the dust collected from the surrounding woollen mills.[2]

A bright girl, Shirley was able to make full use of her expensive education. After boarding at the Heptonstall Academy for the Daughters of Gentlefolk she attended finishing school at Luddendenfoot, before going to Scotland to become one of the first female students at the prestigious University of Lesmahagow. Here she met two of the key figures in her life, her flatmate Dr. Jane Weston, and the man who would chronicle much of her life, Sir Angus Donan-Coyle.

Returning to Yorkshire, she set up home with Jane in Leeds, at 221B Quaker

Ockholmes Lemonade was hugely popular with consumers seeking a flavourful and cheap non-alcoholic beverage, but the lack of a ready supply of lemon trees made the venture a short-lived one.

Street, in the heart of the city's porridge quarter. With a steady income from the browning business she was able to pursue her many interests at leisure. A great fan of licensed music halls, she was nevertheless a strict teetotaller, and spent much time in their kitchen trying to formulate the perfect soft drink, with the aid of tropical fruits grown in a hothouse in the back yard.

Eventually she succeeded in producing delicious lemonade which she marketed for a time under the Ockholmes Lemonade label. When Jane Weston enquired which of the many species in the hothouse had yielded the necessary fruit she was told "A lemon tree, my dear Weston".

Shirley could also be a little eccentric. She insisted that her small office-cum-library be painted bright red.[3]

Her feats of detection were legendary. It was said that she could deduce the brand of cigarettes that a man smoked just by looking at the packet, and could accurately pinpoint the scene of a murder, provided that the rain hadn't washed away the chalk marks. In her most famous case, 'The Affair of the Double Yellow Lines', she brought no less than three North Yorkshire parking offenders to justice, and the grateful folk of Helmsley awarded her the freedom of the town, carrying with it the right to drive sheep over the A170 road bridge.[4]

Thanks to Donan-Coyle, the many other achievements of Shirley Ockholme's career are well known. Nevertheless, it is worth recalling that it was her fondness for music hall that actually brought about her tragic end.

As a regular patron of such legendary Yorkshire theatres as the Leeds City Varieties, the Huddersfield Hippodrome, and the Heinz 57 Varieties (a German-owned chain), she was devoted to such performers as Greasy Folds,[5] Larry Hauder,[6] and Vesta Silley.[7] She was particularly fond of classic music hall numbers such as *Boiled Tripe and Carrots*, *The Boy I Love is Up in Court*, and *It's a Long Way to Thornton Watlass*.

But one music hall performer was different to the rest, and would become Ockholmes' arch enemy and nemesis. I refer, of course, to the evil Professor Morrissey.

Towards the end of the 19th century, a mystery drop in Yorkshire music hall audiences was traced to a curious suicide epidemic amongst patrons. Shirl soon discovered that all those afflicted had recently seen a rising star of the halls – suspiciously, from the western side of the Pennines – by the name of Morrissey. Songs such as *My Old Nurse (Said Follow the Hearse)*, *Daddy Wouldn't Buy Me an AK47*, *I Do Like to Be Sick Beside the Seaside* and *Oh, What a Lovely Wart*, sung in a lugubrious baritone, so depressed the more sensitive in his audience that many lost the will to live.

Suspecting a dastardly plot to depopulate Yorkshire, Shirl went to work. Her pursuit of Morrissey culminated in a final struggle at the top of Bingley five-rise locks, after which neither was ever seen again. Some say both were drowned, others that, in a bizarre twist of fate, they fell in love and eloped to Skipton where they set up a gladioli farm.

We shall never know.

Footnotes

1. Mytholmroyd is notable for being one of relatively few places (outside Wales) whose inhabitants mostly can't spell its name. The natives call it 'Royd'.

2. Initially the product was shipped from the factory by canal, in broad-beamed flat-bottomed barges known as 'Gravy Boats'. With the coming of the railway, faster and more extensive distribution was made possible and with increased production and profits the expression 'Gravy Train' was coined.

3. As recorded by Donan-Coyle in *A Study in Scarlet*.

4. This structure was later immortalised in the classic 1957 J. Arthur Rival film *The Bridge on the River Rye*.

5. Her act, 'Economical Origami', used old fish and chip papers to create accurate scale models of Queen Victoria and Mr Gladstone.

6. Although a fan, Ockholmes is nevertheless believed to have been involved in Hoarder's eventual arrest and conviction for Roaming in the Gloaming.

7. Another novelty act, famed for cooking a delicious Chow Mein live on stage.

MYSTERY IN THE SKIES

For many centuries Yorkshire has been a centre of UFO activity with sightings of strange objects recorded (particularly after 11pm on Friday and Saturday evenings) from ancient times to the present day.

One of the earliest accounts is that of Arthur of Rievaulx,[1] a monk of indeterminate age and dubious sobriety in the 13th century. Arthur records that in the summer of 1245 (or quarter-to-one as it would have been referred to then) a strange circular yellow object was seen in the skies above the abbey on several occasions. The object is said to have been "exceeding bright" and "a little hotte" and only ever made its sporadic appearances in the daytime, during breaks in the cloud.

The mystery of this object has never been fully solved, although some meteorological historians of a sceptical disposition have pointed to the fact that records show the year to have been a particularly damp and gloomy one, even for Yorkshire.

The next major reports of Yorkshire UFOs date from December 1806, when natives of the East Riding began reporting a curious and persistent flashing light low on the horizon. There were many sightings of this phenomenon amongst local farmers, who all agreed that it would cease

The Flamborough Lighthouse: Britain's least successful lighthouse?

suddenly at dawn. But however strongly these tales persisted; they were generally disbelieved by the scientific community, who accepted the evidence of the highly trained keepers of the newly opened Flamborough[2] lighthouse[3] that they could see no such illuminations.

In 1947, a small town near Leeds, was the scene of Yorkshire's most notorious alien encounter, the famous 'Rothwell[4] Incident'. Wreckage was found which suggested that a mysterious craft had crashed in the area, and there were even rumours of strange, almost featureless bodies which were hurriedly removed by 'agents' of Leeds City Council.

Whilst it is now generally accepted that a lorry supplying dummies to Burton's Menswear had merely shed its load, conspiracy theorists are still convinced that someone must have been covering something up, although they are less clear on exactly who, what and why.[5]

Many years later, there came the strange case of Albert Gledhill, of Castleford.[6] Albert claimed to have been doing nothing more than walking home from the pub, when a strange orange glow appeared in the sky ahead of him.

In his own words, "As I walked towards it, it seemed to get nearer and nearer. I realised it must be a spaceship, because it was projecting a strange force-field that caused me to feel extremely dizzy. Then my legs started to wobble. I could see that a strange metallic pole had been extended from the base of the ship, all the way to the ground. I clutched at this pole, and as I did so my legs gave way and I fell to the ground. After that everything seemed weird and dream-like".

Albert described being taken aboard the vessel by two small, shiny aliens whose speech, though reminiscent of English, was strange and difficult to understand. He claimed that these creatures, who identified themselves only as Ent and Dac, then took him to visit their home planet.

It was a strange, draughty place, ruled over by an enormous and somewhat rusty angel. The women (Albert was happy to note) were scantily clad even on the coldest evening, whilst many of the men wore a black and white striped uniform. Regular acts of worship took place in the centre of their city, at a huge shrine dedicated to 'St. James'. For these purposes the men removed their shirts.

Albert remembers little more, and believes he must have been in a trance as the ship returned him to earth. Certainly he was unable to direct them to his home, and as a result he awoke from his stupor to find himself abandoned and clutching at the base of a lamp-post in the early dawn.

Many of the more trusting investigators of this case believe that only alien technology could account for Albert's return trip having taken place in just a single night. Others, refusing to believe that Ent and Dac could possibly be real, take a more sceptical view. The case remains open.

Footnotes

1. Rievaulx was one of the greatest of Yorkshire's monasteries. Although the normal pronunciation is Ree-voe, some scholars suggest that Rye-Vorks is the more correct. It is thought that the 'Rie' is a reference to the nearby river Rye, whilst Vaulx is an alcohol-induced mis-spelling of the former Vaux brewery in Sunderland, only some 50 miles to the north. Hence Rie-vaulx, River of Ale.[i]

2. Flamborough Head protrudes into the North Sea to the persistent inconvenience of unwary shipping. It also has a place in music history, since in 1779 it was the scene of the Battle of Flamborough Head, when a pair of Royal Navy frigates were captured by American ships commanded by John Paul Jones, shortly before he joined Led Zeppelin. This is frequently cited by marine historians as being the only major naval victory by a bass player.

3. This was actually the second lighthouse on the headland. The first was built in 1674 but was never lit. Local historians have long debated the reasons for its relative lack of success.

4. Rothwell is also famous as the site where John O'Groats allegedly slew the last wild bore in England,

although my recent research on Twitter suggests that the species is not entirely extinct.

5. Some suggest that Rothwell's position at the heart of the mysterious 'Rhubarb Triangle' encouraged extraterrestrial visitors. However, the infamous 'alien autopsy' footage, allegedly filmed in a secret military base, is widely regarded as actually showing nothing more than Earnshaw's butchers' apprentices in the early stages of preparing tripe.

6. Generally known as 'Cas Vegas', it is one of West Yorkshire's twin 'Gamblin' Towns', the other being Pontefract, or 'Ponte Carlo'. Cas Vegas concentrates on the casino trade, and Atkinson's Amusement Arcade vies for custom with at least two bingo halls. Ponte Carlo is just a few miles away, on the other side of the great coast-to-coast highway, Route 62. The more glamorous of the two towns, Pontefract is famed for its racecourse, frequently referred to as 'The Ascot of the North', although not necessarily by people from Ascot.

Sub-Footnotes

i. Sworn to avoid any of life's pleasures, the monks also developed an entirely tasteless, flatbread, supposed to sustain life or 'Vita', hence it's name of Rye Vita.

SIR TITUS SHARP

Sir Titus Sharp has something of a mixed reputation in Yorkshire, owing largely to the fact that his natural instinct for acquiring huge sums of money was mixed with a worrying philanthropic streak that he was never quite able to suppress.

Born in Ossett in 1803, Titus Sharp was the son of old Ebenezer Sharp, a woolstapler.[1] Though from one of the less well-off branches of the Sharp family, Ebenezer worked hard and was able to amass enough money to finance his son's education.[2] Thus it was that young Titus was sent to Grammar School, which was where he acquired his reputation for excellent punctuation.

The first half of the 19th century was a period of major growth in the north of England. For example, the population of Bradford grew from 10,000 to 100,000 in this time[3] and other sites were not far behind. In order to provide the growing population with something to do, over 200 factories were hastily erected,[4] and the ready availability of coal, water and sheep in the area led to a huge growth in both the woollen and mutton-broth industries.

With its chimneys continually churning out black smoke and soup-fumes, Bradford, in the face of stiff competition, soon gained the reputation of being the most polluted town in England,.

In 1846, the German poet Georg Weerth[5] wrote that 'If anyone wants to feel how a poor sinner is tormented in Purgatory, let him travel to Bradford', advice which remained in the city's tourist brochures until as late as 1965.

By 1848, Titus Sharp had taken over the family business, owned several mills, and had become mayor of Bradford, in which role his first act was to set up a twinning arrangement with Purgatory, Maine in the USA in 1847.

Tired of combing soot from his not inconsiderable beard, Titus tried to persuade fellow mill-owners to install a mysterious device known as a Rodda Smoke Burner in their chimneys, but it was generally felt that anything which made it easier to actually see Bradford was not necessarily a good thing. Thus it was that in 1850 Titus decided to move three miles to a soon-to-be-former beauty spot on the banks of the River Aire. Here, safely upwind of Bradford, he created a new industrial community called Sharpaire.[6]

At its heart was a great mill, the largest in Europe, as independently certified by the International Guild of Mill-Measurers. Remarkably safe for its time, and incorporating new-fangled innovations such as lighting and ventilation, it was responsible for a significant drop in business amongst local undertakers, leading to a strict work-to-rule on their

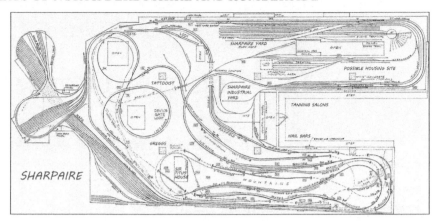

Sharpaire: the original plans were criticised as being overly-dominated by the railway and required major reworking before Sharpaire came to be the place we know today.

part, whereby they would only bury the working class if they were definitely dead.

According to Mr J. Clary, writing in *The Reynolds* newspaper, 'A better looking body of factory hands than those in Sharpaire I have not seen. They are far above the average of their class in Lancashire'.[7]

Sharpaire was designed as a 'model village', a splendid idea in principle, but one which imposed severe restrictions on the maximum height of the workers. Built according to the ideas of Sir Titus himself, Sharpaire had its own school, church, tattoo parlour, pay day lender and even a branch of Greggs. It boasted its own well-stocked library where many a Sharpaire youth learned the now-lost art of searching the dictionary for rude words.

The houses in Sharpaire were far superior to anything working people had previously known. Large enough to avoid the need for synchronised breathing, each house had its own water supply, fortunately, since each also had its own outside lavatory. Amongst other things, this led to cholera becoming deeply unfashionable, and its popularity has never really revived.

Titus Sharp was also active in politics. Believing that the Reform Act of 1832 had one teensy omission (the right of anyone not exceedingly rich to vote) he even went so far as to publicly support the Chartists, and it is quite possible that he may even have drawn some charts for them.

Footnotes

1. This is a trade that has now long died out, following the discovery that no-one really wanted staples in their wool.

2. Although he showed no sign of a willingness to do this until one Christmas when, after a disturbed and sleepless night, he suddenly bought a very large turkey and began generously advancing money to Nigerian princes whose funds were stuck in the banking system.

3. Some authorities suggest this was because the first railway station was constructed without a departure platform.

4. Many were the work of a shadowy character named Jerry Bildt, who may have been an immigrant to the part of Bradford known to this day as Little Germany. Sadly, any record of him must have disappeared when, in the 1960s, it was discovered that there were some handsome buildings left in the city. These were hastily demolished.

5. Georg Weerth was a German writer whose cheery poems celebrated the solidarity of the working class in its fight against oppression. A practical man, he skilfully combined sympathy for exploited textile workers with his role as a sales representative for a textile company.

6. With 'railway mania' breaking out all over Britain, even Sir Titus succumbed to the condition. Fortunately, wiser counsels prevailed before his initial plans for Sharpaire were implemented.

7. Naturally.

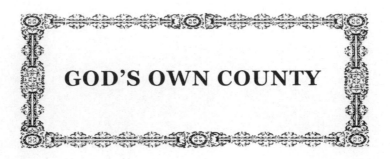

GOD'S OWN COUNTY

Thanks to the sterling work of the small, independent publishing house Yorkie Books, few Yorkshire readers can be unfamiliar with the works of the best-selling author Erich von Kruppenheim.

Untroubled by any considerations relating to accuracy, or even plausibility, von Kruppenheim amassed a small fortune in the 60s and 70s, initially by peddling his controversial and superficially compelling notion that God was a Yorkshireman, the evidence for which had been researched by his own ancient Yorkshire family for generations.[1]

During his many and frequent travels across the county, von Kruppenheim had chanced upon a pyramidal structure in the grounds of Castle Howard, the ancestral home of the Howard family. He was immediately puzzled as to why such a construction should have been built in Yorkshire, and immediately set about discovering the answer. Amongst a variety of theories, he suggested that the pyramid, which sat on a low ridge to the south of the house, had once been used by early inhabitants of the county to worship their ancient gods.[2] But who were these gods, and where were they from? The quest to answer these conundrums became von Kruppenheim's lifelong goal.

The mysterious Pyramid of Castle Howard: an altar for the ancients, or a storehouse for health cosmetics of a somewhat dubious nature?

It was not long afterwards that von Kruppenheim became fascinated by a vast network of primative footpaths and roads that traversed North Yorkshire and which locals called The James Herriot Trail. Even centuries after they were first constructed, the paths continued to draw Yorkshire folk like a magnet, taking in such places as Reeth, Keld, Hawes, Aysgarth and Castle Bolton. Whilst exploring the area, he stumbled on a set of ruined pillars close to Reeth, and soon became convinced that they formed part of an intricate and mysterious pattern of monuments and objects that were linked to the worship of the gods.[3] The stone pillars at Reeth were erected in a long avenue, and von Kruppenheim posited that, when viewed from their western approach, they would line up with the sunrise every year on 1st August. Furthermore, a line drawn due west from the avenue almost perfectly aligned with the apex of Whitby Abbey (using only minor adjustments that allowed for plate tectonics and continental drift). But this was a blind alley - there were no further clues to be had as the line continued out into the North Sea, not reaching land until Denmark, which von Kruppenheim discounted as a highly unlikely home for a god of any description, even allowing for plate tectonics.

The mapping of the ancient pathways and monuments of Yorkshire soon became an obsession for von Kruppenheim. But it wasn't until he had studied his plans for many more months, drawing countless lines across them to bisect places in the hope they might reveal more clues to the mystery, that he finally discovered the answer.

Taking a line from the Pyramid at Castle Howard and tracing it directly to Reeth, he noticed that the path took him through a small market town that was almost equidistant (allowing for continental drift) between the two. The answer had been staring him in the face all along.

Those who were following the James Herriot Trail were wrong - it was to Thirsk, where a separate group of worshippers regularly gathered to acclaim their god - that he must look. Here, in an unassuming terraced house at 23, Kirgkgate was the home of the man who many proclaimed to be God - and he was a Yorkshireman. Von Kruppenheim basked in his discovery for many years, earning a small fortune from books and TV appearances.

It was only when an enterprising researcher from the north east discovered that James Herriot, author, veterinary surgeon and acclaimed Yorkshire God, had

Strange standing stones near Reeth: a place where peat was stored, or a huge terrestrial pointer to Denmark?

in fact been born in Sunderland, Tyne & Wear, that the glitter began to fall off von Kruppenheim's career, but not before he had published another book, *The Black Gold of the Gods*.

Here, von Kruppenheim describes an expedition he undertook through man-made tunnels within the south Ossett district, ably assisted by a local guide named Arthur Bland.[4] He reported seeing mounds of coal, strange wooden roof supports and the remains of a primitive transport system relying on iron rails. Kruppenheim argued that a network of similar tunnels existed all across South Yorkshire and were evidence of an ancient civilisation that worshiped coal. Bland subsequently told *The Leeds Examiner* that there had been no expedition; von Kruppenheim's descriptions came from "a long conversation", and the photos in the book had been "fiddled". During a 1974 TV interview with Michael Parkinsharp, von Kruppenheim asserted that he had indeed seen the tunnels, but he had embellished some aspects of the story to make it more interesting. "In Germany, they say a writer, if he is not writing pure science, is allowed to use some ... theatrical effects," he said. "And that's what I have done." Four years later, he admitted that he had fabricated the entire tunnel adventure, although geologists have since confirmed the existence of many abandoned coal mines in the area.

Whatever one's views of von Kruppenheim's fanciful and frankly ridiculous notions, it is clear that he was entirely unaware of - or, much worse, chose to ignore - an older philosophical tradition in Yorkshire, dating back many centuries, and which was grounded in the works of a now almost forgotten figure, Plaido of Pickering.[5]

Plaido was one of the founding fathers of Yorkshire philosophy (or 'allus bein' reyt', as he called it). He was a pupil of the great Secondrates of Sheffield, who was sadly poisoned by being made to drink southern beer, after criticising Leeds United's back four once too often. None of Secondrates own work is known to survive, but his thoughts live on in the famous 'quarrels', a series of writings by Plaido in which Secondrates pits himself against a suitable dimwit (frequently Lancastrian) in order to demonstrate the superiority of his own thought.

Each of the quarrels was named after whichever poor sap Secondrates was picking on that week, and thus the quarrel in which the nature and existence of God is discussed is the 'Cretinus'. A short extract may serve to illustrate Plaido's style...

The setting is a small village hall somewhere in North Yorkshire (Secondrates was on tour at the time). His aim in this quarrel is to convince Cretinus that God is indeed a Yorkshireman.

We join the debate shortly after the theme tune, and the introduction of the protagonists by Davidus Dimblebore.

Secondrates: And so, Cretinus, look at our surroundings. Look at the glories of Yorkshire. Surely so great a being as God could only have come from this wondrous land? Or are you suggesting that God is (dramatic pause...) a Southerner?!

(Sounds of audience unrest)
Cretinus: I suggest no such thing Secondrates. Rather, I put it to you that only an all-powerful being could have created Yorkshire, as his final supreme expression of all that is good in his universe.
Dimblebore: (pointing) You Sir. The man wearing a smock and chewing a straw.
Man: I blame the immigrants.

We can leave the debate at this point, having heard the first formulation of an argument that has dominated Yorkshire philosophy ever since: was God created by Yorkshire, or Yorkshire created by God?

Secondrates own views were clear, but his work has not aged well, and the sensation-hungry 20th century reader demanded something racier.

Which, of course, brings us back to Erich von Kruppenheim. Despite being discredited by his earlier work, he refused to give up. As noted elsewhere in this volume (see my chapter on Count Dracibird) the pretty fishing port of Whitby is renowned for its surfeit of fish and chip shops. Visiting the town one day, von Kruppenheim sampled a portion, and was immediately bowled over. So much did he enjoy them that he asked himself whether such quality was unique to the town, or if it could be found elsewhere in Yorkshire?

His new odyssey had begun. From Holwick in the north to Totley in the south, Low Bentham in the west, to Kilnsea in the east, Erich von Kruppenheim visited all the fish and chip shops he could find. And to his astonishment, the quality (so he claimed) never varied. Everywhere the same crisp, golden batter, inside which fresh haddock [6] had steamed to perfection, the same greaseless, fluffy chips, the same green and savoury mushy peas.

Even von Kruppenheim might have

struggled to squeeze a book out of this, but there was more. On a visit to Bradford, he was attracted by the aromas wafting from one of the city's countless splendid curry houses. Once again he toured the county, once again he claimed to have found nothing but magnificent masalas, beautiful biryanis, and perfect poppadoms.

All this fired his fertile, not to say overactive, imagination. He began to speculate feverishly as to how such astonishing quality throughout Yorkshire had come about, and these thoughts eventually found expression in his seminal best-seller *Carry-outs of the Gods*.

Here, he returned to the debate that he had so comprehensively lost in *Herriots of the Gods*, now positing not merely that God was a Yorkshireman, but that such was the excellence of their take away food, *all* Yorkshiremen (and women) must, in fact, be Gods.

The Star of India, Ossett - perfect poppadoms.

Reviewers of a southern disposition were naturally inclined to pour scorn on this argument, and neither did it find much favour west of the Pennines. But the book's Yorkshire sales have never been equalled, and thousands of the county's native folk have been driven, reluctantly of course, to the conclusion that Erich von Kruppenheim was correct.

Footnotes

1. Erich von Kruppenheim's father was a German pilot who had been taken prisoner when his Messerschmitt was shot down over Stokesley during WWII. It was whilst working in the fields of North Yorkshire that he met his wife, Nora von Darlington. His claim, therefore, that he had Yorkshire lineage was a typically boisterous one, ignoring as it does the fact that Darlington is on the wrong side of the Tees, and in County Durham.

2. This theory was not comprehensively debunked until 2003, when Dr. Bernice Maidenhoff, Visiting Lecturer in Pyramid Sales at Leeds University, excavated the structure, revealing that it contained a vast store of decomposing aloe vera.

3. Industrial archeologists, geographers and most sane people lined up to dispute von Kruppenheim's theory, but it only emboldened him in his study, even when it was revealed that the stone pillars belonged to a store for peat used to fire the furnaces for the smelting of lead ore at the nearby Old Gang Mill. The stone pillars would have supported a heather thatched roof under which

peat, cut from the nearby moors, was stored, the open sides aiding the drying of the peat. I am sincerely indebted to Dr. W.I. Kipedia of the University of the Bleedin' Obvious for this information.

4. Bland was a member of the 6th Ossett Guides between 1968 and 1971, a time when few but the more enlightened guiding branches would accept boys into their midst.

5. One explanation as to how the town got its name is that a king was passing through one day, and lost his ring in the Costa Beck[i] near the town. He initially accused a beautiful local maiden of stealing it, but later that day was served a pike freshly caught in the beck, and on starting to eat the fish, found the ring inside it. So overjoyed was he that he named the town Pike-ring, which was subsequently corrupted to Pickering. He also, not being a man to pass up a good opportunity, married the maiden.

6. Not Cod. This is Yorkshire.

Sub-Footnote

i. Famed for its dark brown caffeine-rich waters.

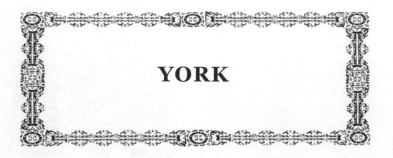

YORK

I have left my definitive account of York until last. Not for alphabetical reasons; if this were a gazetteer Youlthorpe and Youlton would be bringing up the rear. But our tour of the ridings can only end in Yorkshire's finest city (even if it isn't actually in a riding), for within its circuit of ancient walls, history met chocolate in a match made in heaven.

Situated on (and sometimes in) the River Ouse, York was founded in AD71 by the Romans, who named it Eboracum[1] and proclaimed it capital of the province of Britannia Inferior.[2] It was a thriving Roman community but, after the legions left,[3] the city declined until, in the 5th century, it was colonised by the Angles,[4] who, in turn, remained until the Viking[5] invasion of 866.

It was under the Vikings that the city's tourist industry first began to flourish. Encouraged by a succession of benevolent rulers such as Sven Fluffybeard and the mildly bibulous Olaf the Unsteady, a marvellous visitor centre named Jorvik was created, which to this day offers a warm welcome to tourists from as far afield as the USA, Japan and the Isle of Man. However the last Viking ruler, Eric Bloodaxe, seems to have been a less sympathetic character, and was driven from the city in AD 954.

The Shambles in York is actually a street and not, as commonly supposed, a reference to the city's football team.

The Vikings also gave York many of its characteristic street names ending in 'gate',[6] such as High Petergate, Low Petergate, Blue Petergate (named to commemorate a 1973 visit to the city by revered Yorkshireman John Noakes) and Coppergate (the site of York's first police station). The shortest street in York is said to be Whip-Ma-Whop-Ma Gate, which is only fractionally longer than its name plate.

Not having been invaded for some time, it initially came as something of a relief to the people of York when normal invasion service was resumed in 1066. A small rebellion a couple of years later was probably unwise, however - it not having occurred to anybody that someone called 'Edgar the Atheling' might not be a match for 'William the Conqueror'.[7] It was as a result of this unsuccessful insurgence that the first Motte and Bailey[8] castle was constructed on the banks of the Ouse.

There followed a relatively peaceful period, marred only by the trifling matter of the massacre of rather a lot of civilians in York Castle, and some unrest amongst the city's grammarians during the Pedants' Revolt of 1381.[9]

The Minster was built in stages between 1220 and 1472.[10] Said to be the largest Gothic building in northern Europe, it is nevertheless notably deficient in pale make up and black eyeliner. Its famous East Window is often claimed to be the size of a tennis court, a boast that, curiously, is not reciprocated in Wimbledon. Visitors should note, however, that forearm smashes are strongly discouraged by the York Minster Police, a small, specialised cathedral constabulary responsible for policing the building and its grounds.

York's famous walls are the most complete circuit in Britain, and the four main gates, known as barbecues, still survive, although the ancient defensive ritual of getting drunk whilst burning the outside of some frozen hamburgers on summer evenings is no longer practised on them.

A major religious centre, York declined in Tudor times owing to its many monastic establishments having suddenly been dissolved, in history's worst recorded occurrence of acid rain. Nevertheless, it was a York man, Guy Fawkes, who was subsequently found in the cellars of the Houses of Parliament, sitting on a pile of gunpowder barrels and whistling nonchalantly.

In the 18th century, York's importance as a port declined owing to the river silting up. However, the many vessels aground in the Ouse eventually formed a quite impressive-looking marina, and this alone was sufficient to attract the wealthier merchants of the area to live in York. Many of the city's beautiful town houses date from this time, as does the racecourse.[11]

The Victorian era saw two major new industries appear in York: chocolate and railways.

The chocolate industry grew out a famous incident. A local businessman, Sir Terry Katkit, was sitting under a tree in his orchard when a chocolate orange fell on his head. Slightly stunned, he imagined the creation of a chocolate factory where there was was otherwise no logical reason to have one and, being a Quaker, had the optimistic idea that working men might be persuaded to drink hot chocolate instead of beer. Although this latter notion never really took off, the emerging middle classes took to the product enthusiastically, and its future was assured.

The railway industry in York largely owes its existence to George Hudson, the 'Railway King'.[12] His policy of making "all t'railways come to York" was extremely successful for the city, although unpopular with travellers between, for example, London and Brighton. Nevertheless, York remains a major railway junction even to this day, and the National Railway Museum holds the distinction of being the first English national museum to have been built outside London.[13]

York's most recent claim to fame was as the start of Stage 2 of the 2014 Tour de France. This has already gone down on record as the most spectacular collective Sat-Nav failure in history.

Footnotes

1. The origins and meaning of the name are unclear. Some suggest it means 'Yew-Tree', others that it is a word meaning property. A significant school of thought favours 'Buggered If I Know'.

2. This was the northern province of Britain. At one time it extended far beyond the modern Scottish border to the firths of Clyde and Forth, between which its boundary was marked by the Asinine Wall, so-named in recognition of the futility of trying to subdue the Scots. There was also a southern province, based on London, which was known as Britannia thinks-itself-Superior. Female inhabitants were widely believed to wear fur coats and no knickers.

3. The last Roman General in Britain was Magnus Maximus, popular question master of 'Magistersens'.

4. The Angles were a tribe originating in the north of Germany. Under their leader, Pythagoras, they were chiefly noted for the invention of geometry, and were responsible for York's first road sines.

5. The Vikings first announced themselves in England with a vicious surprise attack on Lindisfarne, probably in reprisal for their version of *Fog On The Tyne* with Gazza. This unexpected wholesale bloodshed and slaughter seems to have sullied their reputation somewhat. In fact, recent evidence suggests that they were a much more peaceable and kindly folk than they are given credit for. Their longships were mainly used to take older folk on relaxing cruise holidays, the so-called Viking Sagas.

6. 'Gate' comes from the Norse 'Gata' or 'Gatta', meaning a large sticky cake. Historians have speculated that this indicates that York's confectionary industry is much older than commonly supposed.

7. William's response became known as the 'Harrying of the North', a systematic programme of deliberate destruction of northern communities unequalled until the arrival of Margaret Thatcher in 1979.

8. Messrs. Motte and Bailey were a highly successful mediaeval firm of building contractors. They seem to have been responsible for large numbers of the earlier castles across northern England.

9. The Pedants' Revolt[ii] was led by Which Tyler.

10. In July 1984, the Minster was struck by lighting and badly damaged by fire. Some people were outspoken in their belief that this was a demonstration of divine wrath at the appointment of a controversial Bishop of Durham. They have, though, never entirely managed to explain how Durham Cathedral got away with it.

11. York racecourse stands South-West of the city on an area of land known for centuries as the Knavesmire, from the Anglo-Saxon 'knave' meaning a man of low standing, and 'mire' meaning a swamp. Mud spattered modern-day jockeys of short stature and enduring heavy going have frequently reflected on this naming.

12. George Hudson was farsighted, visionary and a crook of the first order, and thus resembled modern big businessmen in only one respect His career really took off with legacy of £30,000, upon receipt of which he swiftly joined the Tory Party and was elected to the York City Council. He was instrumental in persuading George Stephenson[i] to route the line from Newcastle to London through York rather than Leeds. Unfortunately, his habit of keeping shareholders sweet by paying them dividends that hadn't been earned eventually caught up with him and, in 1849, in the ultimate act of vengeance and punishment, his waxwork at Madame Tussauds was melted down.

13. If any copy of this publication penetrates the M25, readers please note that 'Outside London' is the semi-mythical place it has come from.

Sub-Footnotes

i. George Stephenson is now chiefly famous for designing the revolutionary steam locomotive 'Rocket', which was designed by his son Robert.

ii. The Pedant's Revolt, led by Whom Tyler, took place a year earlier, but failed to attract any support at all.

The Sharps of Ossett

A selective family tree showing the most significant members of the Sharp dynasty.

William Sharpespeare b 1564
Poet and Playwright

Sir Isaac Sharp b 1642
Scientist and Visionary

Alan "Titch" Sharp b 1683
Garden Centre Proprietor

Lancelot "Inability" Sharp b 1716
Gardener & Architect

Admiral Horatio Sharp b 1739
Designer, Peasholm Park

Arthur Wellesley Sharp b 1769
Inventor of Wellingtons

William Sharp the Elder b 1741
Older than William Sharp the Younger

William Sharp the Younger b 1759
Younger than William Sharp the Elder

The Sharp family have always claimed descent from William Sharpespeare. Although no direct evidence for this has ever been found, it would be churlish to let the complete absence of facts get in the way of a good story.

2.

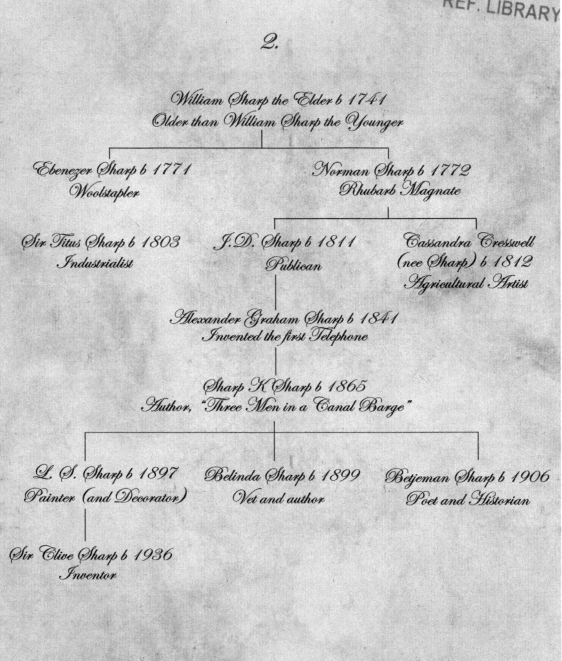

William Sharp the Elder b 1741
Older than William Sharp the Younger

Ebenezer Sharp b 1771
Woolstapler

Norman Sharp b 1772
Rhubarb Magnate

Sir Titus Sharp b 1803
Industrialist

J.D. Sharp b 1811
Publican

**Cassandra Cresswell
(nee Sharp) b 1812**
Agricultural Artist

Alexander Graham Sharp b 1841
Invented the first Telephone

Sharp K Sharp b 1865
Author, "Three Men in a Canal Barge"

L. S. Sharp b 1897
Painter (and Decorator)

Belinda Sharp b 1899
Vet and author

Betjeman Sharp b 1906
Poet and Historian

Sir Clive Sharp b 1936
Inventor

Despite inventing the first telephone, Alexander Graham Sharp's device proved unprofitable until someone invented the second one.

3.

William Sharp the Younger b 1759
Younger than William Sharp the Elder

Mary Sharp b 1790
Knitting Needle Magnate

Sir Mungo Sharp b 1791
Shoddy Manufacturer

Midge Sharp b 1793
Small Businessman

Charles Darwin Sharp b 1818
Author "On the Origin of Sheep"

Cecil Sharp b 1857
Founder of the Competitive Movement

J.R.R. Sharp b 1892
Author and Fantasist

Charles Darwin Sharp completed his treatise 'On the Origin of Sheep' two years after writing 'On the Origami of the Species', which failed to achieve wide distribution after the publisher folded.

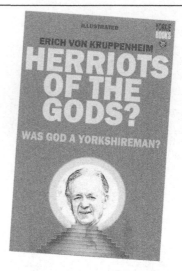

ABOUT THE AUTHOR

Eric Kirkheaton Shipley yields to no man, and very few women, in his love of Yorkshire. His fascination with his native county has been with him since his earliest days, when his grandmother would sit him on her knee and regale him with indigenous tales and legends in her thick Holmfirth accent. Unfortunately it was so thick he couldn't understand a word she said, and had to go down to his local library to read them instead.

These early visits were to instil in him his other great love; books. He was lucky enough to achieve his childhood desire to be a librarian whilst still a young man, and his happiest days were spent travelling the highways and byways of Yorkshire in various mobile libraries. With his knowledge of the county thus increased tenfold, he settled down as Deputy Librarian of Ossett Library, a post he held until his retirement.

Finding himself with plenty of time now available, he pursued his greatest ambition, to combine for posterity his twin passions for Yorkshire and books. The result, you hold in in your hand.

SELECT BIBLIOGRAPHY*

Betjeman Sharp: The Poetry, the Lorries and the Art — Sir Miles Mawsking-Taype

Myths, Legends and Downright Lies of Yorkshire — Stan Broker

Yorkshire Plowrights: A Brief History — Orson Carter

Come on baby, light my fire! Yorkshire Fire-Lighting Habits in the 1920s — Wath-upon-Dearne Historical Society

Stuffing My Face: A Brief History of Snacking — S. Barrass and C. Walker

Cage Fighting for Toddlers — Josiah Scarlazzi

Yorkshire Mud: An Adult Colouring Book (includes free brown felt tip pen)

Friday Night, Saturday Morning — Alan Stilleto

Monday Night, Tuesday Morning— Alan Stilleto

How to Write a Bestseller — Alan Stiletto

The Arthur Conquests — Alan Aysgarth

The Woman on the Tram — Alan Bennite

* All titles currently out of print unless otherwise stated.

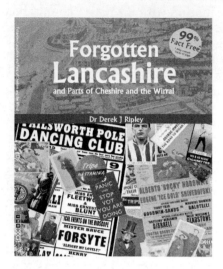

FORGOTTEN LANCASHIRE AND PARTS OF CHESHIRE AND THE WIRRAL

The book that launched the TMB's reputation for Fact Free History. Dr Derek J Ripley makes a brave stab at throwing light on one family's contribution to Lancashire history.

'Comic genius or woeful local history'
Lancashire Life

'A dozen laughs a page'
Wigan Observer

'The antidote to local history books'
Linghams Books

'Not quite what I expected!'
Theresa Tracey, Four Star Amazon Reviewer

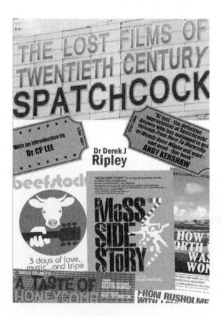

THE LOST FILMS OF 20th CENTURY SPATCHCOCK

Dr Ripley turns his attention to a detailed appraisal of Alfred Spatchcock's Oldham-based film studios.

'Anyone who has managed to get through From Here To Maternity or Wendy Does Wigan will want - and need - this book.'
Andy Kershaw, Broadcaster

'Hilarious!'
Billy Butler, BBC Radio Merseyside

T M B
BOOKS

MY CAMEL'S NAME
IS BRIAN

Goole-born primary school deputy head teacher Jonathan Humble brings us this widely-acclaimed collection of his humorous verse, which takes a wry look at life through his spectacles.

'wide-ranging, inconspicuously thought-provoking and undoubtedly very funny.'
Helen Perkins, North West Evening Mail

TALES FROM
THE TILL

Our lightest 'tripe' book yet—only three references to tripe! Bill Cawley's one-man mass observation survey lifts the lid on life in a modern supermarket.

'Think short snappy twitter style tweets. Little nuggets of wit and fun and nostalgia and empathy.'
AKA Rod, Five Star Amazon Reviewer

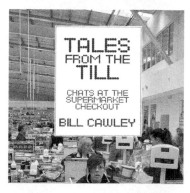

A BRIEF HISTORY
OF TRIPE

More than you might ever want to know about the history of tripe and the marketing of this original wonder food*, complete with the first ever history of Tripe Club.

* Most people wonder why anyone eats it.

All our books are available from Amazon and direct from the publisher at
www.tripemarketingboard.co.uk/books

Coming Soon from TMB Books

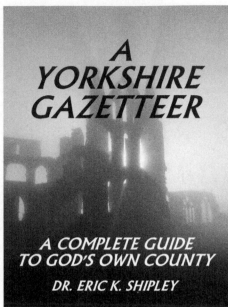

Dr Eric K Shipley brings his unrivalled knowledge of Yorkshire to bear on the cities, towns and villages of Yorkshire.

***A Yorkshire Gazetteer* will be a book to own and treasure for years to come.**

W

Wakefield
The City of Wakefield has been extensively redeveloped in recent years. A number of the city's architects were involved in an innovative guide dog sharing scheme.

Wales
The village lies in the far south of Yorkshire, on the Derbyshire border. Happily, it is small in size so expenditure on bilingual road signs is minimal.

Walkington
This East Riding village is best known for the nearby Walkington Wold, a remarkably well preserved bronze age barrow, with its front wheel still intact.

Wetherby
A town of old coaching inns, roughly midway between London and Edinburgh. Those in the know still mourn the passing of Wetherby Racecourse oxtail soup.

Whitgift
Despite having a lighthouse 20 miles inland, an area of Whitgift, and nearby Ousefleet, was nevertheless officially identified by the Ordnance Survey as the dullest place in Britain.

A

Clapham—

Acaster Malbis
Not to be confused with Acaster Selby.

Acaster Selby
Not to be confused with Acaster Malbis. So named because in Norman times the village was brought under the control of Selby Abbey by one Osbert de Arches, of Ambridge, Borsetshire. He was celebrated in song by Flanagan and Allen.

Acklam (Middlesbrough)
Not to be confused with Acklam (Ryedale).

Acklam (Ryedale)
Not to be confused with Acklam (Middlesbrough). The last village to be founded before the principle of recycling names to save money was found to be fundamentally flawed.

Addingham
Birthplace of Sir Clive Sharp, inventor of the calculator.

Agbrigg
...old suburb, once known as Sandal ...me was dropped when it ...are common

Aldfield
The closest village to Fountains Abbey. As a result, subject to flooding when the wind is in the wrong direction.

Altofts
Birthplace of Elizabethan navigator Martin Frobisher. His descendents roamed the continent with tape measures until they were able to establish that, in Silkstone Row, Altofts had the longest unbroken row of three-storey terraced houses anywhere in Europe. It was demolished anyhow.

Angram (Harrogate), Angram (Richmondshire)
These two villages are Angrams of each other.

Arkendale
The name is believed to derive from the Old English "Eorcon", meaning to make cooler, and the Viking "Dale", meaning valley.

B

Baildon
Baildon is home to the Frances Ferrand memorial fountain. This is known locally, for no readily apparent reason, as 'The Potted Meat Stick'.

Bardsey
Bardsey is an ambitious village, claiming to possess both the first Anglo-Saxon church tower in England, and the country's oldest public house. Its boast that it is also a small island off the coast of Wales is generally disregarded.

Barnoldswick
A controversial inclusion in this list as technically the town is in Lancashire, and has been since the Local Government Disorganisation of 1974. However, the previous 1,000 years having been spent in Yorkshire, it is included here. There are frequent proposals for an exchange of prisoners, involving the return of Todmorden to Lancashire.

Printed in Great Britain
by Amazon

12429120R00061